## PRAISE FOR OOPS! THE PARE

Erik R Robertson, with his extensive experience anu expertise in counselling, offers practical, easy to follow solutions to help parents bond with their children better in a simple, pleasurable, yet rewarding manner. His system of using warm as well as strong guidance will help both families in crisis and families who want to avoid troubles. He brings practical knowledge for new age parents in the form of amusing anecdotes, Action Plans, and Points to Ponder. Thus, an immensely readable book is also a workbook, a toolkit, that will help all parents understand the principles of raising happy children into confident adults, who know how to live in and develop positive relationships with those around them.

**DR. ROMA KUMAR, MBBS, MA**, Senior Clinical Psychologist, Ganga Ram Hospital; Founder Saksham, psycho-educational services for children with special needs

Erik R. Robertson's Oops! The Parenting Handbook is a refreshingly different, practical parenting toolkit from infancy to adolescence, with a baseline of values and a touch of spirituality, in just over a 100 pages! Rather than providing a pure discourse in psychology, Robertson jogs up what we already knew 'intuitively' as caregivers but was hidden under layers of cultural conditioning. He tries to brush off these layers to tell us – hey! Trust yourself, and pass that trust to your children. With you 'love' and 'law', they'll do just fine.

**V.K. PARSAI**, Family Psychotherapist, Member Executive Body of the Indian Association for Family Therapy

I met the author by chance on a retreat in Sedona. I flipped through his book and was immediately impressed! As a mother of 7, I can appreciate the information he presents in an easy-to-read, no- nonsense format. I will be including his book in the hand out material of all my child birth education classes. A+ book!

**Anonymous**, Amazon Review

As a parent, I can highly recommend this book as it offers guidance, which has very obviously been well thought about and one can also detect, that a lot of love and care have gone into researching this extremely important subject matter. Our children are our future, therefore it is extremely important that we raise them and teach them with as much informed knowledge that we can possibly gather. This very readable and educative book does just that. Many grateful thanks to Erik Robertson for his work.

**Anonymous**, Amazon Review

I had the pleasure of reading "oops the parenting handbook"! This is a must read for every new parent coming home with their new bundle of joy. I used to joke with friends and family about parenting my now adult children, "let me go check my manual" I would say! I had no manual! Most parents are left to just wing-it on gut instinct when it comes to parenting. I wish I would have had this wonderful book that Erik Roberson so brilliantly has written. I highly recommend it to all people who are parenting kids!

**Julie Musial**, Wisconsin, USA

Being a Paediatrician for 25 years, and an author of three parenting books, Oops came as a surprise. Erik writes with tremendous clarity and purpose. He's got his basics on parenting bang on. What makes Oops different from many other parenting books that I have read, is that the underlying matrix of Oops is spirituality, and is based on the fundamental and simple human values of honesty, openness, trust, commitment to children and family, and a genuine desire to better the future course of humanity, by bringing up a better, stronger and well balanced breed of children. Oops holds the seeds for the future of a peaceful and harmonious human existence. I feel that every man and woman who wishes to be a parent should read and understand this book much before he has children, so that the tools and ideas are already in place, when the baby arrives. I wish Erik and his book all the very best and am hoping to see it on the bestseller list soon.

**Dr. P. V. VAIDYANATHAN. M. D**, Paediatrician
and Author, Mumbai, India

Your book came to me when I needed it the most. It taught me how to deal with teenagers – something which no other book explains as beautifully and as easily. Thank you for bringing my children back to me.

**R.M.**

And they lived happily ever after…" This is a common feeling of hope…Hope to grow up as beloved persons. This book gives such practical tools for parenting… the base of our child-hood… in communication and more. A great small (120 pages) book Erik! Well done.

**Ellen Rose Van Oord Van Westrenen**

Erik Robertson's big heart for the well-being of children is what you will feel during reading this wonderful book. And aren't we all children? That's how magnificent his heart IS! Please let yourself be inspired by the deep wisdom of this very well-educated, experienced, very conscious and loving man! Your life and that of your child(ren) will never be the same anymore!

**Jacqueline Lammerts**, Counsellor, inspirator and
author for all the children of the world.

*I wish I had
known this before...*

# THE PARENTING
# HANDBOOK

Erik R. Robertson, M.A.

**BALBOA.**
PRESS

A DIVISION OF HAY HOUSE

Balboa Press books may be ordered through booksellers or by contacting:

Balboa Press
A Division of Hay House
1663 Liberty Drive
Bloomington, IN 47403
www.balboapress.com
1-(877) 407-4847

**Disclaimer:**
The information in this book is in no way to be taken as advice per se. As a parent, you remain entirely responsible for the implementation of your parenting. The author/publisher is in no way whatsoever responsible for the contents, and neither is he responsible for the given information and suggestions. The author is free now and forevermore from any legal actions and/or prosecution.

For specific help with parenting problems, you will need to consult your physician, local health services, and psychologists.

In the case of serious psychological problems, you might do well to consult a psychiatrist.

Because of the dynamic nature of the Internet, any web addresses or links contained in this book may have changed since publication and may no longer be valid. The views expressed in this work are solely those of the author and do not necessarily reflect the views of the publisher, and the publisher hereby disclaims any responsibility for them.

The author of this book does not dispense medical advice or prescribe the use of any technique as a form of treatment for physical, emotional, or medical problems without the advice of a physician, either directly or indirectly. The intent of the author is only to offer information of a general nature to help you in your quest for emotional and spiritual well-being. In the event you use any of the information in this book for yourself, which is your constitutional right, the author and the publisher assume no responsibility for your actions.

Printed in the United States of America.

ISBN: 978-1-4525-8084-5 (sc)
ISBN: 978-1-4525-8086-9 (hc)
ISBN: 978-1-4525-8085-2 (e)

Library of Congress Control Number: 2013915393

Balboa Press rev. date: 01/05/2015

## DEDICATION

I dedicate this book to every parent
to help you celebrate being the best parent that you can be. *Oops!*
*The Parenting Handbook* will support and empower you!

# Contents

# Acknowledgments

*I am grateful and indebted to all whom I have met. My heartfelt gratitude goes to all those hundreds of thousands of parents, families, and children I have been allowed to serve, and who have trusted me with their lives.*

*I am grateful to all my teachers, both spiritual and academic. Thank you for your patience, love, and knowledge.*

*Thank you to all those countless education professionals all over the world for sharing your experiences with me, and thank you to all those professionals out there doing your beautiful work every day.*

*I feel infinite gratitude for my own biological parents, grandparents, and ancestors.*

*I express my gratitude to all nations of this wonderful planet as well as to Mother Nature.*

*I wish to thank deeply all at Balboa Press and Hay House.*

*Thank you to those few precious people who will remain unnamed – you know who you are. Thank you for always believing in me and guiding me forward!*

Erik R. Robertson
*Amsterdam*
*27 June 2013*

# Foreword

You have made a wise decision in obtaining of copy of Erik's book on parenting. It is extremely relevant and timely to our times. We are witnessing high and rising rates of depression, anxiety, conduct disorders and other serious mental, emotional, and behavioral problems among children and adolescents globally.

What is causing this crisis? It is our lack of connectedness with our spiritual selves – our own inner values and worth. This makes us unable to transfer this experience, this direction, to our children.

To realize that we are divine beings playing a human role in the drama of the world and not humans trying to be divine, the only obstacle is the mind, and there is only one way – connecting and loving God more and more. If parents truly love God, spiritually centered children with discipline and character will be the natural byproduct.

Added to this is the responsibility to use the secret- "believe what you want to happen has happened". As the parent's thoughts play a defining role in a child's future, parents must always look upon their children by their potentialities and not by the comparative analysis of their current performances. Management is really about making others realize their potential through creating appropriate circumstances. Management of the lives of children is no different.

In this context, the story of Edison is a wonderful example. When Edison was sent back home with a comment by the teacher that he is too dumb to learn, his mother said, "My Tommy is not a dumb – I will teach him myself". The result of that positive perception was that the world got an Edison that changed the world for the better, forever. Thus parents must realize that God has given them two ears and one tongue so as to listen more and advise less, to understand more and impose less.

Yet, some children bring forth their innate tendencies from past lives or gather them from other environments, and may hence exhibit behavior that challenges their inherent potentialities. To execute a course correction, parents must put into practice knowledge of two fundamental concepts of life (1) The *Karma* theory – as you sow, so shall you reap. Hence, if the parents constantly sow love and hope in the hearts of their children, it will eventually destroy the weeds of hate and despair (2) Treat children as children of God – be not possessive yet positive. Let me substantiate the virtue of non-attached love of parents in this context by means of a small story narrated by Sri Sathya Sai Baba.

Once there lived a couple with their two virtuous sons. But unfortunately, one day they both died due to a disease when their father was away. The mother on his return accosted him and said, "Dear one, a long time ago a saint had given me two priceless jewels for safe keeping. When he came and asked for them, I felt very sad and miserable." The husband replied, "Dear one, do not fret as these jewels went back to where they belonged. But tell me what these jewels were?" The wife then takes the husband to the dead bodies of their sons and says, "These, my Lord were these two jewels that God has taken back".

Now, to treat our children as children of God, we would first have to treat ourselves as embodiments of God. If you were to try and define God in a single word, it has to none other than Love. But what is the nature of God's love? God's love is infinitely selfless, expansive and deep, and it is in that direction that parent's love has to proceed. As God could not be everywhere, He created parents to share His love with all His creation. So the main job of parents, especially the mother, is to shower the child with all the love at her command.

As fruits and flowers of a plant cannot be sustained without watering of the roots, this love cannot be sustained unless the parents exhibit intense love for at least one of the five fundamental values professed by all societies and religions worth their names, i.e. truth, righteousness, peace, love and non-violence. More than mere verbal articulation, the need of practical exhibition of these values is the need of the hour and these five values are interlinked inseparably. For example, to get peace based on untruthfulness, unrighteousness, hate and violence is unimaginable!

Thus as parents, it is our duty to sow the seeds of such values in the hearts of our children that they live for a goal that is high and generous, broad and disinterested. Parents must make children understand the need for short-term sacrifices for long run peace and bliss, by their own example.

If education for a child starts in the lap of the parents and the end of education is good character, parents are their first teachers. Yes discipline is important in these times of immense distractions, a strong hedge is required around the sapling in its tender years, but a child needs to outgrow the hedge and find his true potential. The most feared medicine in the mind of the child should be denial of the pure and pristine love of his parents and this should arouse the inner voice of conscience to live up to their noble expectations.

I am sure that Oops! The Parenting Handbook will be a guiding light to all parents who love their children and are concerned about their well-being and their future. This book will equip you with an inward-outward approach to secure a life of peace and prosperity for your children. It will empower them through you to have a better tomorrow - a tomorrow that is valuable to them and to all society as they leave a glowing legacy for their children and grandchildren.

Dr. Deepak Anand
Assistant Professor
SSSIHL (Deemed University)

# A Preface To Oops!
# The Parenting Handbook

*Am I doing things right?*
*How will I keep this up?*

This is not the umpteenth book on parenting. *Oops! wish I had known this before* is a synthesis of four decades' worth of knowledge and wisdom on this topic. *Oops!* amalgamates academic points of view and methods on parenting with holistic and spiritual perspectives.

Far from an all-encompassing piece of work, it is, however, a parenting aide, an invitation to learn a collective wisdom. It is here to help you, support you, inspire you, and cut through the huge mass of contradictory advice that is out there in the media today. *Oops!* contains the essence of all the best parenting practices and methods, in the hope that it will reduce parental insecurity. It is for those moments of struggle and despair and confounding times when you ask yourself, *What kind of parenting style is right for me? Authoritarian? Permissive? Authoritative? Am I doing things right? How will I keep this up?*

While writing the first edition in 2011–12, research revealed that, in the Netherlands alone, during the first half of the year, the number of requests for parental support increased by 30 per cent compared to the previous year. Similar data can be found in most European countries. Colleagues to whom I have spoken in various education-related fields in the United States tell me it is the same there. In many western European countries, the average waiting time to see a professional trained in child developmental problems is anywhere between four weeks to four months or longer. Experience shows us that it is highly practical and meaningful to develop awareness about parenting prior to and during the role and duties as a parent. It is of crucial importance to pay attention to these matters. The parents-to-be feel better equipped to fulfil this fantastic and sometimes difficult task.

There is a tremendous amount of pedagogical literature available, ranging from books to various magazines on parenting issues. All this can be informative and entertaining. It is, however, the predominant cause of a great deal of parental confusion on how to be a good parent. Not all sources are online. Because the media keeps updating its databases on research findings and constantly refreshing them, I have based my statements on my professional experience in various international areas of educational psychology gained between 1997 and 2013.

Confusion does not do your parenting any good. Children want and need clarity, consistency, and love. And clarity is related to boundaries, rules, self-confidence, and an absence of doubt. If anything goes wrong, the label *problem children/youth/families* is quickly tagged on. The term *problem families* is offensive and derogatory. In my opinion, there is no such thing as a *problem child* or *family*. There are only children, teenagers, or families going through difficult situations and needing help and support to stay on track.

This book has been written full of love and respect for you as a parent, with a heart full of comprehension, empathy, and compassion for the complex challenges and problems you face. It is meant to accompany you as you cherish the joys and endure the pangs of every micro-moment of your child's safety and well-being as Nature's most important gift, the ability to beget, and sustain life itself. Oops! is an energy book. Readers have reported that they have felt touched and stimulated to grow in ways they had not thought possible. But mostly, it is here for you during all those wonderful and exhilarating blissful moments of love that you and your children will be sharing!

*Oops!* will help you prepare for parenting and then fine tune your existing parenting skills. And when your children are older, this book will be there when you self-reflect. It will help you to be kind and gentle to your real (and imagined) weaknesses. As a parent bombarded with dos and don'ts from all fronts, the sceptic in you is wondering... *Am I capable of making this work? Do I have enough love and wisdom within me to make this work? Can I ever be, a successful parent? Oops! The Parenting Handbook* will help you to shape and give depth to the love, knowledge, and self-confidence that is already there inside you. It will support you in your pursuit of development and excellence.

Our world and community are growing more and more complex. To be able to handle this well as an adult, you and your children will need love, *love, and more love,* and, of course, *rules and structure.* Love speaks for itself. Love is acceptance and appreciation for who you are. It also encompasses warmth, support, comfort, compassion, understanding, tolerance, patience, and unconditional love for your unique being. Love is humour, fun, shooting the breeze, and playing too. Rules and structure go hand in hand with love and are interrelated. Structure and rules offer safety and clarity. Rules teach a child to learn to deal with frustration as well as the conditions of others. When becoming an adult, it is necessary to be able to cope with the unavoidable frustrations that life will place in your path. The rules at school and traffic rules are prime examples of the never-ending rules that society has invented – not to mention taxes!

I believe that holistic parenting advice is all around us – in the music we hear, the experiences we choose, the authors we read, and the people we encounter. My sources of inspiration are wide and varied. They include various religious and spiritual schools of thought, meditation and wellness....

- love
- Sri Sathya Sai
- J. Krishnamurti
- Apple
- the Beatles
- Yogananda
- the Dalai Lama
- Buddha
- the Findhorn community
- wealth
- animals

- dolphins (a highly evolved species)
- spiritual seekers from all over the world
- life
- SSSIHL
- Sir Paul Smith
- Sir Winston Churchill
- the angels
- Babaji
- Baba Neem Karoli
- India
- Harrods
- butterflies
- Mother Earth
- Etro
- Mahatma Gandhi
- Oprah
- Hawaii
- Glastonbury
- children
- ladybirds

*Oops!* was written with an ambitious mission: that humanity sees a glorious new generation of parents who will benefit children here and now, and thus consequently, the human species. The future of the world depends on this, as your children will be the shapers of our future world. This is an enormously fun yet serious challenge, and it depends on you – no more and no less! And yes, you and your children, armed with love and respect for each other, are going to make this beautiful journey a successful one with a very happy ending! This book will support a new generation of beautiful heroes: your children!

With deep respect,
Erik R. Robertson
*Amsterdam, The Netherlands*

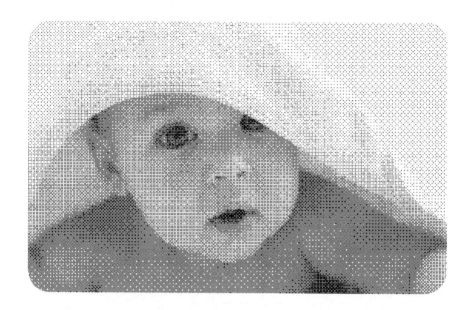

# CHAPTER 1

# Learn From Your Baby

Oops! Suddenly, you're the parent of a tiny being who is a complete mystery to you, someone for whom you feel so much love and on whom you have no grip whatsoever.

Welcome to the world of parenting – to your new life as a parent.

Forget about all the parenting books, websites, and blogs that you have read so far. Forget all the well-meant advice given by your parents, grandparents, colleagues, and neighbours.

Your child has one message for you, and it goes as follows: 'It's between you and me now, buddy!' In other words, 'We are now both in unfamiliar territory,' meaning that your child will be using you and your partner as guinea pigs and for target practice in developing his or her unique genetic and karmic package (or character, if you will).

Further, your child will mirror you to an extent that will be quite disconcerting and, of course, amusing and endearing, as well. He or she will mirror all that you are repressing (that is, all your unconscious behaviour). These are the things you had long forgotten, including your own hidden childhood traumas and discomforts and all emotional matters that you manage to rationalize for yourself. Why? Because, for the baby, there is only the here and now – a world of feeling and eternal now.

If babies could somehow communicate how the world looks and feels to them, and how they interact with the world, it might go something like this:

- No thinking. No worrying. No insincere behaviour. No faking. An ocean of bliss.
- What I feel is what I feel, and that is what I share in my purest and most virtuous form.
- And further, I sense and suffer all that you feel and/or suppress. I am who I am. No compromising (yet). I am either happy or unhappy, or I am in that delightful, pure now, where things simply are.
- So there is no need for you to distract me or for you to entertain me. My cognitive abilities and my development will start up by themselves, because my brain is programmed to develop at lightning speed.

As loving parents with only the best of intentions, we all tend to make serious mistakes that may have huge consequences at a later stage. The biggest mistake is projecting our perception of reality onto our baby or child. This will lead to a myriad of problems later in life.

Because each generation of new souls on this planet – and each new baby – has his/her own *programme* to follow, the less we interfere, the more successfully it can unfold. Parenting is all about facilitating and being a good example.

In contrast to most adults, a baby's world is one big party (unless of course when suffering from teething, growing pains or sources of stress from outside of them). Babies are learning about the world all the time, and they do this without any outside help. It is furthermore interesting to note that education is such a historical and cultural construction.

# POINTS TO PONDER

*Live now!*
*Do this by emptying your head.*
*Be more like your baby. Just be.*
*Observe, feel, and listen.*
*Be yourself.*
*Work on yourself.*
*Strive to be at peace.*
*Babies do not need to be entertained.*
*Learn from your baby.*

# CHAPTER 2

# Let Your Baby Play and Dream

Nowadays, we are inundated with thousands of books on parenting and hundreds of magazines and websites, all of which overemphasize the early cognitive development of children. In doing so, these resources (perhaps inadvertently) ignore the most important aspect of being human: the fact that we are already whole at birth. Our soul and its wisdom are present and available.

I do not wish to imply that the brain has no need to develop and train itself. Of course it does. Further, all kinds of talents need to be developed so that they reach maturation and perfection.

Due to pseudoscientific research (and mostly due to vested commercial interests), we as parents are overloaded with *educational* games for our babies. And babies certainly do not need to be subjected to the myth that the games on the iPad will help them to develop more quickly. (This is suggested by some biased and uninformed individuals and, of course, by the companies developing these apps.) The tablets can be great tools if they are used wisely. On all fronts, we are advised to start with their development as quickly as possible.

I am not in favour of this. It is unnecessary, and experience shows that the longer babies can play, the quicker and better they develop later on. Though vast numbers of therapists and educators all over the world share this experience, there is regrettably no longitudinal research to prove this... yet!

This focus on early development does have some positive aspects. When the development of the intelligence of a baby is started at a very young age and applied diligently, the child will be years ahead of her peers later on at school and in college. The development of intelligence is not per se the same as early cognitive development in the strict scholastic sense.

I am referring to mothers who will speak to their babies several times daily, explaining to them what they are doing the same way they would to an alien visiting Planet Earth for the first time. It seems that when doing this diligently, and at the same time allowing for plenty of play, these children go through school much more quickly and easily than others who have not had this *treatment*. Equally important, specific music will aid in sleep and in brain development. There are many websites dedicated to this, so I will not quote any for risk of sounding biased.

However, during a baby's first years, a loving and safe environment is the most important thing because it allows the baby to be herself, to have lots of time to play, and to enjoy and relax. That is the best approach, as the baby will learn the most – yes, just by playing.

Many geniuses stress the importance of playing and daydreaming in their childhood, and they continue to do so as adults.

> *Play is the highest form of research.*
> Albert Einstein

As parents, we need to be highly alert when it comes to interacting with our babies. For example, if my baby is stressed and unhappy, I should check to see if I and/ or my partner are unhappy or stressed.

Please note that when the word *partner* is used, it is not suggested there is or has to be a partner. All situations described throughout the book are applicable to all forms of parenting, be it single parents, divorced couples, same-gender parents, extended new families, et cetera. If we both relax, the baby will relax.

Of course, as parents, it is hard to relax because we are biologically programmed to be alert around babies. Almost every mother knows the nights of light and restless sleep because one ear is listening to every sound her baby is making.

Fathers are much less burdened with that instinct, though of course, they can be extra protective. With fathers, the difficulty in relaxing can manifest itself as wanting to take care of the family by protecting the nest financially through hard work.

But is all of the above enough when we are asked to be 'highly alert' in our interaction with our children? Yes and no, though mostly no. In many cases, most (if not all) of the educating or upbringing is quite straightforward. However, in far too many instances, many things go horribly wrong due to a lack of knowledge on the part of the parent, for example, leading to all kinds of problem behaviour, violence at home, failure at school, drugs, alcohol, auto-mutilation, and suicide.

You understandably do not know what you should be alert about. You are trained extensively for almost everything in life, yet for the most important task-Parenting- you are expected to get by. And, on the other hand, you are too busy to have enough energy left to be highly alert. Modern life is, after all, unbelievably fast-paced and overwhelming.

In fact, the pace of our modern culture is opposite to that of a newborn and preschooler. To begin with, they live in a world that is completely defined by food and sleep. Meanwhile, their minds are eager to the point of being anxious and are ready to develop.

However, in order to develop effectively, a nurturing environment of love and peace are essential. In fact, this is more essential than the use of constant images and learning experiences that the salesmen of computers would have you believe are necessary.

An example from my practice illustrates the complexity of the early years as I have shared above. A wonderful, charming, and successful couple came to me for counselling. Their four-year-old daughter, had the most violent temper tantrums. To the horror of the parents, she would bash her head often. When the mother served dinner, she had a habit of taking a plateful of hot food and hurling the food (as well as the plate) across the room. Imagine your favourite cream-coloured new sofas and rugs covered in spaghetti sauce!

The parents understandably had no idea what to do, and as head bashing can be psychiatric in nature and they were terrified of seeing the school psychologist, I decided to work with the parents on their own issues: confidence, strength, loving authority, and so on. A few weeks later, I had a sobbing mother on the line, joyfully exclaiming, 'I have my sweet little girl back.' It was very touching. No more head bashing, no more throwing around dinner plates!

It is not enough to create a safe place and evaluate our own stress levels to be successful in our parenting. If you think I might be biased or overly negative, think again. I am basing my statement that *very often many things go wrong in parenting* on an endless stream of expensive, and for the most part, useless reports that have been published on this matter over the last three decades in the Netherlands and most northern European countries.

I value and appreciate all the reports and data that have been generated worldwide by concerned education research, be it academic or investigative in nature. I call them useless because they are very costly, and they keep coming up with many similar conclusions: there is an increase in violence at school and at home, more and more children are dropping out, and there is a decline in grades and in basic skills, such as reading, writing, math, and common knowledge.

Schools and colleges are swamped with increased government demands on all kinds of control systems. This is basically governments telling schools that they do not trust them. All this extra bureaucratic work is at the expense of money and time spent on the student: your child! And yet, basically very little changes. The rapid change in our societies over the last five decades has had tremendous impact on the family. Families face problems in coping with these changes. As a result, every nation has more troubled families than necessary, not to mention the harm that is done.

Experts tell us (and I concur, obviously) that stress among parents is directly responsible for all manner of behavioural problems: sleep disorders, ADHD (attention deficit/hyperactivity disorder), ODD (oppositional defiant disorder), learning problems, addictions, and so on. And certainly the abovementioned problems can also have genetic and environmental causes as well. It is usually a cocktail of many different factors.

Help is available. There are numerous parenting courses (including my own proven effective workshops), therapists and counsellors who specialize in parenting issues, as well as educational psychologists – the latter are to be found in most, if not all, schools. At the first hint of problem behaviour in your child, you should immediately contact these professionals who can help you set things straight before matters get worse and slowly spiral out of control.

Parental discomfort or embarrassment can lead to the question that many marriage therapists as well as educators know only too well: Why did you wait so long before seeking professional help?

# POINTS TO PONDER

*Review how you as a child*
*experienced your own parents.*
*Who are the role models you have*
*integrated into your own parenting?*
*To what extent is there peace in*
*your life and in your home?*
*How can you make your life*
*more 'baby friendly'?*

# CHAPTER 3

# Focus on What You Can Control

Informative media tells us that unacceptable behaviour in babies and children is the direct and irrefutable consequence of a lack of awareness on the part of parents, as well as an inability to cope with their own problems, barring of course, specific unresolved physical problems and/ or genetic issues that result in behavioural problems.

I strongly argue against the cliché of *quality time versus quantity time*, which is a gimmick used by way too many educators, magazines, websites, and authors to sell a new gimmick to parents. For babies and young children, there is only *time*, not this flash of so-called *quality* time! They just want your time and attention without you being distracted by your tablet, phone, PC, and so on!

Furthermore, parenting requires listening and taking time instead of criticizing and correcting. The two former aspects require lots of time, and the latter are often the result of being rushed or unclear about rules and boundaries. We will go into this later on.

It is either that lack of awareness and self-knowledge or the stress of negative parenting practices that is the root cause of so many so-called *problem families*. Many educational psychologists and several case studies vouch for this fact.

Family dynamics is a complex issue, and it would take a whole book to explain the intricacies. Suffice it to say that when becoming a parent, you subconsciously dredge up all your own negative and positive parenting experiences, as well as all your previous interactions with authority figures.

As soon as you become a parent, issues of power and control (and the lack of them) come up. These are often reinforced if you have a partner and/or are raising your children with others. All kinds of murky feelings related to lack of control, fear, and powerlessness pop up. Babies and young children sense this, and they do not like it! Before you know it you, your baby or child, and your partner are involved in subconscious and unconscious power struggles, fears, and games, all of which limit your effectiveness as a parent.

Now, please understand, there is no judgment in this statement. I certainly do not judge you as a parent. This stuff just happens to many parents! You love your baby/ child, and you read all you could before they were born and then suddenly you feel helpless and lost because nothing prepared you for all these feelings and issues. I totally understand that and empathize with you! This is why I place enormous emphasis on building awareness, self-knowledge, and love! This counteracts the above-mentioned negativity.

To paraphrase Mr Miyagi, 'No bad children, only "bad" parents.' I put the word bad in quotation marks because I do not believe there is such a thing as bad parents (exceptions to the rule being parents who abuse their children in any manner). Parents have problems because of a lack of awareness, which is mostly due to a lack of information or knowledge because no one tells us how to prepare for this most important life event.

When you become parents, you most likely had little or no training for parenting, and the knowledge that you did have was probably made up of a large assortment of mostly contradictory advice found on the Internet, offered by friends and parents, and read in magazines, books, and so on. Imagine wanting to build a bridge and hiring an architect and some engineers whose qualifications consisted of some weekend courses in architecture or engineering. Would you hire these guys? The strange thing is that we are trained for everything in life except for the most important task that exists: parenting. With this task, we are expected to *make do.*

And make no bones about it… parenting is, unquestionably, our most important task. This is because it has such a large-scale, societal, moral dimension. The quality of

> *Leave your children alone, and work on yourselves*
> J. Krishnamurti

your parenting today will determine the quality of your nation in the future – no more, no less.

For now, though, it probably feels like you are on your own. As I explained before, the home arena is a place in which you will need to find your own way of coping with parenting. Of course, my own or other parenting workshops can be of great help here, but they only go so far. Your home is a private domain where you need to develop your own unique parenting style and skills.

Our world as parents consists mostly of meetings, traffic jams, our weekly planner, our greed, our stress, our moods, and being 'busy, busy, busy'. We have no time for the delays, the nagging, or the complex problems that raising a baby or pre-schooler can entail.

The following story is an example of the failure of many parents to engage with their children. Instead, those parents criticize their child's behaviour or attempt to correct it – interactions that can be devastating to the children.

It was a radiant spring day, and I was walking back from the beach. Up ahead of me, I heard a dad calling out to his adorable, fairy-like young daughters. He was apparently visiting them on the beach, wearing a business suit and carrying a briefcase. They had understandably been clamouring for their father's attention, and he responded by saying,

'And now, it is time for you to stop whining.' These sweethearts were trying to tell Daddy what they had been doing that day! *Ouch*!

My guess is that they were three or four years old, and they only wanted to do one thing: share their joy and enthusiasm with Dad, whom they had missed all day.

By responding as he did, we do not create children; we create neurotic monsters. Their shocked, sad, and confused faces remained etched on my retina all the way home. The scene broke my heart as he broke theirs with his shouting and lack of love.

Little souls who are full of love have only one reference point and that is Mommy and Daddy. Their parents are gods for them. Everything in their lives, certainly in the first years, will be decided by these *gods*.

Children are wired with certain beliefs about their parents' interactions with them. Here is one of these:

*When Daddy or Mommy criticize my natural and loving behaviour, then there must be something wrong with me.* This is how little children think (and how these girls reacted), and how you and I responded when we were small.

Children have two other unusual and illogical types of programming that determine their entire being: *If Mommy or Daddy has a problem, then I need to fix it.* Even worse is the sentiment: *It is also my fault if they quarrel or fight.*

Please take this to heart and let it be a serious warning to keep as many of your problems as possible out of your children's lives, since children have a natural antenna for such problems.

There are several ways that parents can accomplish this. For instance, you can learn deep breathing. Just the simple act of taking a few deep breaths can be enough to get your heart rate and adrenaline down after a long and tiresome drive home. You can curb your urge or desire to immediately react to a problem with your partner and agree to use a certain prearranged signal that you will both address the problem later. This approach shows that the two of you will act as one and that you are united in your common parenting goal. This should not be too hard, because you love your children!

Reality, however, is more tenacious. We are so highly individualized and often obsessed with the importance of our egos, opinions, emotions, and thoughts that our individuality takes over negatively instead of letting our wisdom, souls, hearts, and love preside! Easier said than done, I know, but this is the real work parents need to engage in!

If the father from my previous example had had even half an ounce of usable EQ (emotional intelligence quotient) in his head, he would have lovingly told these girls that he was happy that they wanted to tell him everything. He could have briefly explained why he could not or would not do so at that very moment, and that he would listen to them at such and such a time. Even a simple 'Wait, dears' would have been appropriate.

The girls would have been reassured that they were loved, and that the situation had nothing to do with them – *it had to do with Daddy.*

In handling situations in this manner, we will create a new generation of children who are open and well balanced emotionally. On the other hand, people who behave in the manner of the dad in question, will create insecure, neurotic children, even though the love the parent feels for the children and his or her best intentions cannot be doubted.

When these children become adults, they will take all criticism personally (does this sound familiar?) because their parents made all their criticism personal, instead of keeping it impersonal.

Using language consciously to ensure that the way we talk to our children lifts them up rather than crushes them will make a world of difference in our relationship with them, and more importantly, in their peer relationships as well as in their inner world.

Avoid using aggressive blaming and shaming messages (such as, *You are so slow* or *You are a klutz*). These are personal attacks. Children will internalize them, and the effect of these attacks will manifest in negative behaviour and beliefs.

Instead, use neutral 'I' messages: *I am displeased when you complete this task so slowly* or *I am unhappy that you broke the vase.* These messages are helpful and far less harmful. They guide a child without implying that something is inherently wrong with him or her.

Here are some examples that do much more damage, which is really bad because it is emotional terror (sometimes well meant): *You are really dumb, You are so clumsy,* or *You always get that wrong, silly.*

But as the saying goes, the road to hell is paved with good intentions. Why are those last expressions considered to be so damaging? Because for a young child whose brain and subconscious are like a sponge, and who sees his or her parents and teachers as gods, every criticism is taken very seriously and literally so they really hit home – hard. And a child generally lacks the capacity to defend himself or herself against criticism.

They lack the objectivity to realize that the criticism is unjust and not personal and that it says something about the person expressing it. (Though some kids are so wise and together that they are able to distance themselves and not take it personally).

For children, the previous examples are extremely personal. In their own perception, they are for the most part (if not entirely) dependent on their parents and their approval for survival. This means that they have an enormous need for positive feedback, reinforcement, reward, and recognition! I will address this later on in this book. Negative criticism or feedback is destructive if given in the previously mentioned manner. Supportive criticism and feedback, on the other hand, are good and even necessary.

There is a huge difference between *You are so stupid* and *That is a stupid way to do something*. In the first case, there is a clear judgment; in other words, what they do is who they are. For a small, developing human being, this is awful! And unfair! However, when you discern between who they are (good, sweet, and fun) and what they do (in this case, according to you, stupid, bad, and clumsy), then you give them a chance to look at their actions without losing their personal dignity.

When giving feedback or criticism, what also works well is to *first start off* by telling your children what you think they do well and what pleases you, *then* add explain what you feel is wrong or could use improvement. You should make it clear that your criticism is just your value judgment – no more, no less.

I think back to the beach that day, and I see those two lovely girls clam up, on the verge of tears and devastated because of their father's harsh and harmful words. I feel and share their pain. At that very moment, I sent them a warm, loving smile, which I saw register briefly through their tears. I can only pray that this might have helped them realize they were loved.

The ancient Chinese called *angry words more lethal than poisoned arrows*. Of course, the girls would soon forget the incident and would be giggling again in a while, but it is the constant accumulation of verbal abuse and the emotional immaturity of the parent that leave their mark.

I have seen many, many sad examples of the above in my own parenting practice. Basically everywhere I go, I see daily examples of parents shaming and blaming their children… sad but true. This manifests in children as insecurity, self-doubt, macho behaviour, nail biting, substance abuse, addictions, phobias, autism, and so on. The list is endless. Autism is a complex matter. Medical experts tell us it can have a genetic component. However, it is my experience that autism is often the result of the highly sensitive and/or strong-willed baby in question not feeling understood, welcome, or loved! This can be compounded by aggressive and excessive verbal behaviour on the part of the parents. When this behaviour is remedied, I have seen astonishing changes for the better in some so-called autistic children.

Academics and professionals will hasten to point out that the abovementioned list cannot be related to the parents, but is instead related to the genes, the character of the child, the social environment, and so on. This is partially right, of course, but experience shows us that if it is your intention to bring about practical improvements, it is best to focus on what is within your own span of control – your own behaviour!

In the next chapter, we'll examine more ways that we can ensure we are providing our children positive, constructive feedback.

# POINTS TO PONDER

*How do I handle criticism?*
*How do I express criticism?*
*What is the effect of my voice*
*(and opinion) on my children,*
*partner, and myself?*
*How did my parents express*
*their criticism to me?*
*How much and how often do I*
*internally criticize myself?*

# CHAPTER 4

# Harness the Power of Communication: Nonverbal and Verbal

The upbringing of children is not so much about the child, but about the parent! It is all about *your* behaviour, because *your* behaviour will determine the behaviour and development of your child. You can trivialize or deny this statement all you want; however, it does not change the truth of it.

As parents, we can sometimes be prone to feeling overwhelmed by guilt and inadequacy because we think that we are *not doing it right* or because children are masters at manipulating us to make us feel guilty. Furthermore, as parents, we may feel angry or fearful about our lives in general. These feelings can then influence the way we communicate with our children and thus begin negative cycles of parenting. So it is very important that you compliment yourself for all the great work you do every day. In this way, we can build positive cycles of parenting.

In addition to a child's inborn character traits and his or her genetic programming, your child will, for the most part, be shaped by your behaviour, by the example you set. Later on, teachers and peers will also contribute to this example function.

It is a well-known fact that an adult conveys almost 85 per cent of his messages through nonverbal signals. With young children, this is probably almost 95 if not 100 per cent! Certainly during the first years before they learn to speak, it is mostly nonverbal, and then as they learn to speak, verbal messages gain in importance. Yet, most educators feel that children learn mostly by watching, copying, and modelling behaviour of parents and peers!

## Developmental psychologists have always known children learn by imitating adults.

Think about it. They learn by copying what they see and hear. Therefore, all that we wish to see in our children, we will have to model as good examples. In addition to that, all verbal statements that we make are a direct order for our child – a direct link to his or her subconscious.

## Give YES messages, not DON'T messages.

Many parents are always surprised as to why their children fall down when moments earlier they had so adamantly warned, 'Be careful that you don't fall!' If I tell you not to think of a pink elephant, what happens? Right, you will visualize nothing but a pink elephant. So do you see what happens when you give your child a do not instruction? Exactly. As I said earlier, it is all about awareness. Use it or lose it!

So how does it work to your child's advantage, and how will you as a parent successfully reach your goal? By giving a yes message. Then *Be careful that you don't fall* becomes *Be careful when you run*. Or just plain *Be careful*.

Forewarned is forearmed. So say, *Remember your keys* instead of the often used, *Don't forget your keys*. This is very practical advice for adults as well because you don't realize that you keep forgetting things only because you are constantly conditioning yourself with not messages. In training yourself to change do not messages into yes messages, you will automatically extend the same good habit to your children.

Words like *always, every time*, and *constantly* are not welcome. They have a very negative effect and should be avoided.

Unlike 99 per cent of all adults, a young child is totally present in the moment. In the *now*. Incidentally, this being in the here and now (nowhere/now here), is what all spiritual aspirants strive for. And this is what we find so attractive in children, in addition to their frankness and their unconditional love and purity. By addressing a child with *always, all the time*, and *constantly*, you force that child to not be present in the moment, and you constantly force old bad memories onto him or her.

Memories of previous failures and humiliations will then overpower the child, and the child then reacts negatively. We often make it worse by saying things, such as *Grow up, Don't be such a baby, Look at your brother/sister, they know better,* et cetera.

For those of you who think you do not really use these negative words a lot, I would like to invite you to keep score with your partner on how often you really do use them (or think them) in the course of a week. You will be amazed.

This is also a great exercise that you can practice in your relationship. How often do you address each other with these words?

If you are single or in a relationship, you can also practice awareness of how often you unconsciously address yourself with these negatives, such as *See, there you do it again, You are always so slow,* et cetera.

The words *always, each time*, and *constantly*, are terribly powerful mantras. In addition to these phrases, there is also the *yes, but* where we're just making our own points rather than hearing and validating those of the others. These are followed by an endless list of explanations, justifications, clarifications, and excuses.

In order for us to truly listen to our children, we first need to stop – to completely stop – what we are doing. This means stop our busy minds, turn off the electronic devices, and then just be there for our child. Then, chances are you will find yourself actually listening.

Do you catch yourself formulating an answer before your child has finished speaking? This means you are *not* listening. Are you matching what you hear to your own experiences? You are simply *not listening!*

In this age of so-called communication, we hear all too many people complaining that we are communicating less than ever. In reality, one could say that without awareness, what is happening is that:

- We hear, but we do not listen.
- We look, but we do not see.
- We talk, but we do not say much.

These are only a few examples of the power of words and of how you can shape the subconscious of your child for positive educational purposes. You can learn more about this method by checking out (among other methods) NLP (neurolinguistic programming) online.

## *Practice awareness to receive treasures.*

Our parenting – especially that of young children – is a fantastic invitation to work on our awareness of ourselves, our children, life, and our conditioning, and to become aware of the beautiful experiences that are the true treasures we share with our young children. To find and receive these treasures, it is necessary to be awake and alert. We must see them, hear, feel, and discern them.

Sometimes, the packaging is extremely unattractive. It may take the shape of annoying behaviour, defiance, rebellion, sadness, anger, and disease. Nevertheless, awareness is crucial if you want to make your parenting successful! If you pay attention to only the unattractive, undesirable behaviour of your child – or worse, if you *identify* your child with his or her behaviour – chances are high that you will get mired in negative parenting cycles.

Looking past the behaviour will enable you to get back to the essence of the issue, and then when necessary, you can always correct such behaviour at a later point in time. It takes strength, awareness, love, and courage to master this sometimes highly challenging task of being a *super human.*

In addition to becoming more aware as parents, we also look for practical tools, and we will talk more about these further on. However, in order to let your actions lead to the desired results, you will first need insight.

# POINTS TO PONDER

*Are you aware of your actions?*
*How is your nonverbal behaviour?*
*Are you paying attention to your*
*breathing (or the lack of it)?*
*Count how often you smile every*
*day. How often do you frown?*
*How often are you angry? Why? Are you*
*angry with someone else? With yourself?*
*How often are you afraid? Why?*
*Where does the fear come*
*from? What does it do for you?*
*Is there another way for you to*
*react? What does that do for you?*

# CHAPTER 5

## Love and Law

Taking into consideration the enormous number of how-to books and the constant stream of *experts* telling us that everything can be learned, it is understandable that, as a parent, you go looking for tools. And this strengthens the thought that, as long as we learn enough skills, we will have what it takes to be a good parent. And here lies the problem.

Sure, many skills can be learned, but if you recall our discussion of a young baby in the first chapter, you are dealing with a unique, unpredictable, and uncontrollable phenomenon. *Uncontrollable* is used in the sense that there are no skills that can help you here as a baby or young child will simply mirror all of your traits, including your less-attractive ones, your hang-ups, and your suppressed feelings. And this is because children are very impressionable, pure, and true to what they feel.

We also looked at the unconscious dynamics that tend to sneak into all family dynamics, whether you are a single mom or dad, a married couple, divorced, or have an extended family. There is only one way to develop skills and that is to be a good example of all those good qualities you wish to see in your child.

During the first years of life, your child will be learning only by observing you very closely, by sensing what you are feeling. He or she will then mirror and copy your behaviour. So, if you do not like what it is that your baby is showing you, then take a good look in the mirror.

In fact, we all know that this mirroring and copying is how it works. Haven't we all seen young and/or first-time parents especially enjoy sharing hilarious anecdotes about the bad or funny words and expressions that their young offspring have picked up (from them)?

Of course, this can be hilarious as well as very endearing; however, you are missing the opportunity of a lifetime if you do not look past the funny side of this behaviour. You now have a unique chance to use this uncanny and accurate *copycat* behaviour of your young children to teach them what it is that you feel they need for their development!

Regarding specific tools, there are a certain number of tools that you yourself can develop as well. In doing so, you will be transforming your self-knowledge and insights into a broad range of capacities. It is my vision and experience that you can place all your capacities and knowledge into two categories: *love* and *law*.

All the success that you can imagine (and need) as a parent will be yours by applying these two principles and by developing the abilities that are related to this.

### Unconditional love is unconditionally the only love we must nurture.

When we talk about love, parenting is continuously challenging us to go deep within ourselves and to search for that source of unconditional love within one's self.

That unconditional love is something that we will need on a regular basis. We will need it when our child's behaviour almost drives us to despair, when our feelings of powerlessness rise to heights that we did not think existed.

As human beings, our love is almost always of a conditional nature. I love you as long as...

- you act in this or that manner,
- you do so and so,
- you do that for me in return,
- you love me in return,
- you show me that you love me too, et cetera.

It is harder to love unconditionally during moments when your baby or child acts in a most unreasonable manner – when he or she screams so loud that it wakes up the neighbours, when he or she doesn't want to eat or to sleep, and when that child pukes all over you and your belongings, and of course, when you have refused something to your child in every possible way and he or she sees this as an invitation to begin incessant manipulation and game playing. You feel that your child has outsmarted you, taken over, and is onto you.

These are the moments that your love diminishes and sometimes seems to disappear altogether. The moment you think or notice that you have stopped loving your baby or young one is when things go from bad to worse. It is then that you also stop loving yourself. The door opens and in walk self-criticism and insecurity, as well as the related fear, anger, and rage.

And that is not a good place to be. In other words, you are in a state of mind that benefits no one, least of all yourself.

### Unconditional love begins with unconditional acceptance of ourselves and our children.

This leaves us with only one option: giving unconditional love, which at difficult moments like this is akin to unconditional acceptance of yourself, and more importantly, of your child or baby.

Your baby/child needs you. A very, very large percentage of the previously mentioned unwanted behaviour of the first years is directly related to you and to what your baby senses is going on with you.

Of course, some situations are more complex, and some unwanted behaviour may relate to physical discomfort. We, as parents, must ensure that our children's physical needs are met and that they aren't suffering from some type of infection or some other physical ailment.

Psychologically, on the one hand, your baby will want to test you, see what you are made of, figure out your boundaries, and find out what is acceptable. On the other hand, negative (unwanted) behaviour is often related to problems that *you* are having. A baby or child can only communicate his or her discomfort in a single way – by being a nuisance.

Think about all the programmes on TV about this topic or think back to those difficult moments in your own parenting. As soon as parents are well balanced and well organized (and if need be, have worked through their issues), then most problematic behaviour is either absent or rapidly diminishes.

Furthermore, a baby has no verbal repertoire to speak of. Unlike adults, a baby can't sit down at the kitchen table and have a good heart-to-heart with us. When children and babies express themselves in what we label as problematic or annoying behaviour, we set out to solve the problem as quickly as possible and we tend to do so by engaging in a power struggle, and that is a tactic that has no winners.

## *Use behaviour to avoid power struggles.*

When we find ourselves *battling* with such behaviour, we should take a step back, take a deep breath, and rethink the situation.

When we lock into power struggles with our children's behaviour, we tend to diminish our own control. Our child enters a battle of wills with us because on the one hand, that is natural developmental behaviour, and on the other, the child is testing the boundaries to see if we will be the positive authority figures he or she needs us to be.

When we are in a good space, we can see these struggles (which are generally about not wanting to do what we have decided needs to be done!) from a mile away. However, we might be feeling tired, low, sad, stressed, or we may just plainly be doubting our own authority or decision-making. Wham! That is when our children instinctively sense an opening and dive in. Hey, wouldn't you? You probably did the same when you were young.

Suddenly, we find our interaction with our children to be fierce ego against fierce ego! Our child might be mirroring our upsets or vice versa. At moments like these, you need to be really aware, and as soon as you see the pattern, know and trust that you are halfway toward recovery.

Observe yourself objectively. See yourself having these feelings, and think hard about the reason why your baby or child is doing this. Depending on his or her age, you can engage in some verbal dialogue (befitting the age), or you can use your intuition and feelings to figure out what is going on.

There is definitely a way that prevents you from becoming overpowered by your feelings of powerlessness, of being carried away by fear and rage and only you know it. Experience teaches us that these feelings almost always lead to verbal and/or physical violence, which always leads to feelings of guilt and regret. Further on in this book, I will address the dangers of becoming overpowered by feelings of regret and guilt.

To avoid falling prey to this spiral of powerlessness, there is one fail-safe tool at your disposal: law.

## *You can rescue powerless parenting by laying down the law.*

When we talk about being strict, and even more intense, the importance of consequences and punishment, then something strange happens. We start to feel uncomfortable.

Punishing and rules are often considered to be old-fashioned. They have become most unpopular since the fifties.

*When you are not strict when necessary, then your action or inaction is loveless.*

I will say it again. When you are not strict when necessary, then you are not being a loving parent! Said differently: when you are strict when necessary, then you are a very loving parent.

We usually think the exact opposite: *If I am strict, I am mean, and therefore, unloving.* Be it conscious or subconscious, this is a deep-seated conviction many parents have. When this conviction gets linked to feelings of guilt, the result is most harmful because children have an antenna for these emotions, and they tend to internalize them. They feel responsible for the adult's feelings and begin to have those very same adult feelings about themselves. So the guilt children sense in their parents becomes guilt within themselves.

Furthermore, they know in their hearts whether their actions are good or bad. They also know when strictness, punishment, or consequences are called for! Most young children between the ages of three and 10 are overly strict with themselves when it comes to deciding appropriate consequences for their own transgressions, so it is something you need to decide on, after discussing with them what they feel is needed.

When you as a parent do not have this same moral compass in good working order, you are letting your kids down (in their perception). So, it is of the utmost importance to be able to be strict when it is necessary. You have to be able to take a stand and also to enforce consequences and punishment when needed! This is a non-negotiable aspect of good parenting!

## It is possible to punish with unconditional love.

There is one prerequisite for administering punishment: make sure that your heart is full of love, *unconditional love.*

We tend to associate being strict and enforcing consequences or punishments with previous generations that would (at times) do so without love or discernment. That is why I emphatically state that punishing only works when done from a point of deep love.

## Rules allow you to manifest your own boundaries: Negotiate punishments with children

Being clear about your authority as a parent is a tool that you can and need to use to guard and/or manifest your own boundaries. In addition, there are some more conditions.

As soon as your child is old enough (age varies from child to child), it is best to negotiate consequences and punishment with him or her.

You will be amazed how harsh children tend to be toward themselves and the consequence or punishment that they feel they deserve for unwarranted behaviour. It then becomes your role to modify their harshness and help them make the consequence/punishment fair and proportionate to the misbehaviour. In this way, you teach them the importance of forgiving themselves and others. They learn how to administer kindness, compassion, and understanding when dealing with themselves and others.

Parents have a better perspective on how commensurate the punishment is to the transgression. Parents know that punishment or consequence is not the goal but only a necessary tool designed to help our children grow into responsible strong adults. Children, on the other hand, deal with themselves with an intensity that needs a parent's balance and equanimity.

There is another reason that consequences/rules/ boundaries are so very important. For many children, boundaries that are clear and negotiable offer great security. As long as the boundaries are unclear, a child will keep pushing and continue provoking until the boundary/limit is clear. Pushing boundaries is also important; by no means am I ignoring the fact that the healthy exploration of boundaries in necessary for the brain to develop. Later on, in puberty, this aspect will play an important role. However, for the moment, let us address the necessity of having boundaries at all.

These enable you to manifest your authority in a natural manner. As long as you do so with respect for the intrinsic equality of you and your child (which by the way is not the same as the two of you being equal), then all is well.

In doing so, you prevent yourself from disempowering yourself, from being without authority, and from being unable to do that for which you have been *appointed* – raising your children.

## Lack of boundaries lands older kids into trouble.

One of the reasons that so many teenagers end up as juvenile delinquents is that they finally discover a boundary at the point of becoming a delinquent. There should have been several boundaries well before this point. But since there were none, tragically, it takes a jail cell to manifest the ultimate clear boundary. A jail does not yield or give in, and in jail, rules are rules!

It does not necessarily mean that these teenagers consciously seek out this situation. On the contrary, if more parents and educators had made more effort at an earlier stage to be stricter and at the same time more loving, then – as one often sees – it might not have had to come to this.

Furthermore, the world of criminal gangs is extremely clear about rules and boundaries. Their acceptance is often unconditional, as is the love in whatever form it may manifest itself. And love manifesting itself as acceptance is what teenagers have an inexhaustible need of. While it is not my intention to exalt criminal gangs, I do want to draw attention to the importance of rules even in this most unlikely of places. Breaking rules has enormous consequences in the underworld, leading to severe punishment – even death.

The lesson here for families is that you can forge strong bonds and become united, provided you take two matters highly seriously: love (unconditional acceptance of each other, and loyalty!), and law (rules and boundaries as well as the related consequences). From this clearly established base, this code of conduct for your family, you can then create a common family identity, a strong bond, and clear characterization of how that defines you. This creates a strong shield against the outside world that, due to an increasingly fast culture and loss of values, has allowed negative influences on family life to proliferate.

There are more specific tools you can use to make your parenting stronger, more loving, and more *effective*. For those who might have problems with the word *effective*, by this I mean that you, as a parent, are not just able but actually empowered to give your child all that your loving heart wants him or her to have. As a parent, you have the ability to pass on to your children those values that you would like them to develop and embody.

# POINTS TO PONDER

*How do you handle boundaries?*
*How do you feel about love and law?*
  *What aspects do you want to use*
  *to empower your family?*
*How will you be an inspiring*
  *example for your children?*
*Make an action plan in order to*
  *discuss with your partner how clear*
  *boundaries give a solid base for*
  *your children's good development.*
*Regularly evaluate together what you*
  *are both doing and what you radiate*
  *emotionally; and more so, evaluate*
  *the effect on your children.*

# CHAPTER 6

# Empower Your Family with Human Values

Today's hectic pace, as discussed previously, makes for increased pressure on our family life.

Our education systems implicitly and explicitly place a huge emphasis on competition, materialism, and getting ahead. Good and necessary as that may be, things are out of balance.

Education is also all about developing our character, gaining self-knowledge, learning about mankind, and opening our hearts. I therefore feel that education should be called *educare. Educare* contains the word *care*. Sounds warm, doesn't it? This is how education should be – enabling the child to develop and manifest his or her own inner wisdom and beauty.

Human values are the most powerful tool you can use to improve yourself to empower your family and to make the world a better place for all of mankind.

There is a dramatic increase in violence in schools – and everywhere in society for that matter. I recall giving a human values workshop at a school in the Netherlands somewhere in the 1990s. At that point,

European parents were a bit concerned about increased reports in the US media about shootings at schools. The parents present at the workshop were convinced this was an isolated US situation. I calmly told them that, notwithstanding my everlasting optimism, they were wrong and that there could be violence of that same nature at our schools, both at the middle school as well as the high school levels.

Regrettably, I was right. The last decade in Europe has been rife with stabbings, death threats to teachers, shootings, killings, and increased violence of every possible kind. Documentation of these tragedies is available in old news records of almost every European nation.

The number of suicides amongst students is increasing in many nations. The number of students who have taken their own lives in England and Wales has increased dramatically since the start of the recession. Between 2007 and 2011, suicides by male students in full-time higher education grew by 36 per cent, from 57 to 78 suicides, while female student suicides almost doubled from 18 to 34, according to new figures released by the Office for National Statistics (ONS) (http:// www.guardian.co.uk/higher-education-network/2012/ nov/30/ student-suicide-recession-mental-health).

Many psychiatrists and psychologists report a whole new target group in their practices – primary schoolchildren with stress and burnout symptoms. Let me repeat that. *Primary schoolchildren with stress and burnout symptoms are unable to cope mentally.*

To stop this escalation of violence, inhumanness, stress, and misery, human values are much needed.

Fighting against violence is completely futile. And by *fighting*, I mean you must refute violence completely, becoming an activist against it, and so on. But there is something else that you can do.

When you enter a dark room, what do you do? Do you start yelling and shouting that there needs to be light? Do you send a letter to your congressman? Of course not! You switch on the light.

Perhaps it is a funny example; however, it is the most appropriate one of the fight against violence. The only remedy is to *turn on the light.* In our case, this means the application of human values.

Because our society is mainly dominated by financial values, it is a good idea to balance that out by explicitly using some human values.

Almost everyone has some idea of what human values are. Usually, respect and peace are mentioned and honesty as well. The Indian leader, Gandhi, was a fine example of freeing an entire nation from a tyrannical and violent rule by the British occupiers through the application of nonviolence and passive resistance.

Most values can be related to five human values that are all interconnected: love, peace, truth (honesty), right conduct, and nonviolence. These timeless values have sub-values, such as respect, and compassion.

*Right conduct* might be doing *the right thing* depending on your role in life, as well as *doing your duty* or *doing what needs to be done*. As the saying goes, *it is a tough job, but someone needs to do it*.

*Love* has other values contained within it, such as kindness, compassion, and empathy.

*Peace* can include patience, open communication, less verbal violence toward each other, et cetera.

*Truth* can include being honest and speaking your own truth.

*Nonviolence* can include less cursing and being kind to yourself and others. Nonviolence as a feeling is peace, and in speech, it is truth.

Parents can sit down with their children and discuss together how they feel about these five values and how they, as a family, can apply these and other values. This can be done in a manner that suits your family lifestyle.

Those families that actively invest in applying human values experience more happiness and fulfilment in all areas of their lives. I personally know of several schools in the UK, India and in the Netherlands that explicitly apply the five human values in their curriculum. All staff, parents, and children have reported that student behaviour has improved at school and at home, the number of dropouts has decreased, and the grades have gone up compared to previous years prior to the HV courses. Institutes in the UK, Denmark, Thailand, India, and elsewhere also teach human values.

In my own *Love and Law* workshops, I also apply human values as part of the training, and year after year, all parents report vast improvement in the behaviour of their children, immense drops in stress levels of all involved, and a marked improvement in the academic performances of the children. Experience and research also show that children function better at school, have fewer quarrels, are bullied less, and have better grades. Isn't this what everybody wants?

Here are some of my favourite examples of people who embody human values. What names would you add to discuss within your family?

- Nelson Mandela
- Oprah Winfrey
- The Dalai Lama
- Muhammad Yunus of the Grameen Bank

- Mother Teresa
- Martin Luther King Jr.
- Sai Baba

They stood for human values – for compassion, doing the right thing, being there for others, patience, nonviolence, love, and service to mankind. Insight only becomes wisdom when you know how to apply it in your daily life and in parenting.

As for truth and honesty, here is a rather shocking example from a survey called 'Parents bribe their kids', in the United Kingdom (http://www.ukparentslounge. com/According-to-a-survey-Parents-bribe-their-kids-to-keep-secrets-3184.php#.UciXE5wSpc8). Average (English) parents ask their children to keep something a secret 83 times a year! The most used reason to ask for something to be kept a secret was keeping a gift for another family member a secret and lying about a child's age in order to save money. At least five per cent of the interviewed parents admitted that they had asked their children to keep quiet about breaking the law. Most parents admitted to bribing their children up to $200 cash and $250 in gifts annually to guarantee their silence!

The top 10 reasons for asking children to lie are …

*A future gift (54 per cent)*
*Lying about their age for a discount (26 per cent) Staying up too late (22 per cent)*
*Eating junk food or candy (16 per cent) Extravagant purchases (13 per cent)*

*Lying about their age at the movies (9 per cent) Breaking the other parent's rules (8 per cent) Breaking something at home (7 per cent) Breaking the law (5 per cent) Damaging the car (3 per cent)*

These results are quite disturbing, specifically when you relate them to the power of our behaviour and setting a good example. You can be sure that many parents have sugar-coated answers so that they do not come out looking too bad.

# POINTS TO PONDER

*How do you feel about human values?*
*What values do you teach explicitly?*
*Which do you speak about openly*
*in the family circle?*
*What values do you teach implicitly?*
*How would you score on the UK survey*
*as shown in this chapter?*
*Who are your heroes?*

# ACTION PLAN

_____

_____

_____

_____

_____

_____

_____

_____

_____

_____

_____

_____

_____

_____

_____

_____

_____

_____

_____

_____

_____

_____

CHAPTER 7

# Is it Time to Change Our Failing Education Systems?

There are many questions that face us as parents regarding school. Not only is there the question of which school system to choose, but many parents also feel that our current systems need a overhaul. Some even consider the systems obsolete. Should we as parents advocate changes in the education system? Are we not being too complacent by not opting for change? Do we limit ourselves to complaining only when necessary? Are we for the most part being as active as possible in our children's lives, while keeping as low a profile as possible at school? These and many other questions deserve our serious consideration when planning for the future of our children and the future of our nation!

I put forth all this as well as my critical notes further on, with the deepest respect for and acknowledgment of all the wonderful educators worldwide. They are out there giving their heart and soul for our students. The entire period from the ages of four to 18 is for the most part influenced by school, and of course, also by peers and social media.

School has various aspects to it but more than enough has been written about various education systems, so I will limit myself to a general view. While attending school has its pluses, our current education system is failing children in a number of ways. No doubt school is a great opportunity for children but it is perhaps time to recognize that our current education system is by no means making the best of that responsibility. School enables our children to develop their talents and to broaden their knowledge. On the other hand, they are forced into a system that does not pay much attention to the individual. To date, we keep burdening generation after generation with completely useless information – for example, all the civil wars that each country has fought, endless lists of cities for geography classes, and all the great or not-so-great leaders that a nation has had – without making all this data connect or relate to children's own experiences. Knowledge for knowledge's sake has meaning when it is internalized in a personal context. It is far better to equip young children with self-knowledge, insight, and character, and balance this with worldly knowledge.

Or, as the saying goes, *the child first, the pupil next!* The idea is to adapt and to be compliant. For those who need a reminder of the less appealing sides of school, I can recommend Supertramp's hit song 'School' and 'The Wall' by Pink Floyd. As parents, we must ask ourselves some serious questions about our current education system:

- Why do our children have twentieth-century education instead of education for the twenty-first century?
- Why is cooperation and helping each other considered the highest good in the corporate world, yet often forbidden at school?
- Why are the same things explained repeatedly when more than half the students got it the first time?
- Why is competitiveness encouraged so much?

- Why are we so obsessed with judging our children based on their grades instead of their character and other abilities?
- Why do we continue with an education system that insists on passing on information and knowledge that will be obsolete five years from now?
- Why are our children forced to learn subjects with which they have no affinity whatsoever instead of being encouraged to pursue subjects that are in line with their talents?
- Why do children have to learn, learn, and learn instead of being taught to apply, apply, and practice?
- Why do parents keep accepting this often outdated education system that makes so many of our children unhappy and that is debilitating?

These statements are based on the feelings and opinions of millions of students, parents, and educators all over the world. They are the same questions I have heard over a 20-year period, coming from highly motivated, dedicated, and excellent professionals in the fields of education from many different parts of the world. These concerns and critical questions, as well as many solutions, are shared and broadcasted by education pioneers and innovators all over the world.

Here is a case in point. A recent news article teaches us that, over the last 20 years, there has been little or no progress in the field of education. Most experts agree that children worldwide score far below par when it comes to desired and necessary levels of aptitude.

That is why I intentionally use the word *debilitating*. This system is not geared toward their individual talents and qualities, but it limits the mind and channels them toward acceptable standards.

Most of our education systems are based on the needs and thought processes of the early 1900s. But the system is outdated and needs renewal. At the start of the Industrial Revolution, there was a need for various kinds of workers, so the education system started to adapt to the needs of the workplace. This system also contains the elimination principle. Are you unable to participate? Can you keep up? Are you getting in someone's way? Instead, what should have been asked was: *What are your talents? How can we help you develop those talents to their fullest potential?* The education system nowadays, in the Information Age, is pretty much the same as it was back then. Sure, it has had some modifications, and certainly the computer has been revolutionary, but for the main part, it is still the same old system that was used way back then!

That things are not as they should or can be with our schools is obvious to a growing number of concerned people. Thousands of educators and officials repeatedly point out all the shortcomings and the need for change. Then there are the high absentee rates of both students and management, and the alarming increase in violence in many schools and universities. Of the highest concern is the worldwide suicide rate among schoolchildren! In addition to this is the enormous amount of despair and the lack of motivation many pupils and parents feel.

Fortunately, there are more and more schools that realize things need to change. These schools are wonderful examples of innovation and of respect for pupils and teachers. In these schools, students are showered with enthusiasm and support instead of constant correction.

The Sudbury Valley Schools (http://en.wikipedia. org/wiki/ Sudbury_Valley_School) are a great example of doing things differently. Their main educational point is to follow the student/child and learn without coercion!

Not a single subject is compulsory. When one or more students express their interest for a subject and want to learn more, only then do they bring in a teacher knowledgeable on that subject matter. And what are the results of this approach? Students learn the subject in much less time than their peers in regular schools.

This is something teachers in the Sudbury system report time and time again.

The intrinsic motivation, as opposed to having to motivate the child to do your bidding, is what counts. This principle can be applied at any school (and at home for that matter). There is no need to specifically attend this school for that. The tiresome adage that there are so-called learning periods in which a pupil is supposed to be taught, and that if you start too late, there will be a gap that can never be closed, is finally history. Regrettably, this kind of subjective dogma forces millions of pupils to be pushed into unnecessary and frustrating straightjackets.

The first batch of Sudbury Valley graduates shows that the system works: all have jobs, a good income, a happy social life, et cetera (http:// www.education.com/ magazine/article/sudbury-school/). The only demand they place upon their pupils is that they pass their state exams at the end of the year.

The liberal approach is not a free ride. Many people tend to confuse this and other very easy-going approaches to education with a *free for all* ambiance that yields few results. Again, we need to keep in mind my *love and law* approach. Even with all the love and support in the world, rules, exams, and regulations have to be followed!

However, the approach used at the SVS and at other similar schools shows us that, when you leave it up to the student, when he or she wants to learn something, his or her motivation is at its peak. It is then of the utmost importance to follow the pace set by the student and tune in to his or her interests instead of force-feeding him or her in ways that we deem important and necessary. Thank God that more and more similar initiatives are developing all over the world.

If we want a real change of pace in our education system, radical change is necessary. Every year during teachers' training and parenting workshops, I speak to many teachers and parents who are tired of fighting this system. These people have burned out trying to support their children and students to stay true to themselves in this mad system. This includes teachers who are fed up of implementing the umpteenth policy change, teachers who want to teach instead of manage, people in the schooling system who are disillusioned seeing school budgets used up by management teams wasting time, and school principals who have to deal with growing mountains of government paperwork.

I am well aware that there are also thousands of educators who love their work and do it with great pleasure, as well as the many students and pupils who really enjoy school. But the education system is hopelessly old-fashioned and inefficient and has too many casualties.

In the many years that I spent being chairman of an education committee and working with many institutions, I have heard more horror stories than are good for me. The reason for the stagnation of the education field is that you can only successfully change a failing system if you go for a full and total change. When renovating an old house, first everything is gutted – the windows are removed, the wiring is taken out of the walls, et cetera. All that stays up is the framework. Only then can it be rebuilt. New floors are put in, new windows and wiring are installed. Modern and innovative technology is used throughout the house. The result is a new, beautiful house that is relevant to the present era and can be used for ages henceforth.

If you rebuild the house by only changing a floor here or there, leaving the old wiring, after a few years you will have a serious problem. The building will be about to fall apart, and you will need to start all over again.

Strangely enough, this is how we go about our education system. 'This is highly illogical,' as First Officer Spock would say. It is not smart; it is short-term thinking, and the avoidance of risks is due to fear of real change. It is all very human and understandable; however, it does not serve our evolution!

Since we appear to live in a democracy, it is up to you as a reader, as a parent, as a teacher, as a school director to inform our politicians and government that we want a different system.

### *Our most important duty towards our children is to help them build their character.*

The single most important duty of school is the development of good character, and that children learn to develop their hearts – the previously mentioned aspect of *educare.*

Children can learn from the ageless wisdom that has been passed down from generation to generation in all cultures. We need to enable children to understand what it means to be a human being. Children should be taught that we are unique in creation and that we have the capacity to think and analyse and to be able to distinguish right from wrong behaviour! That is the only thing that separates us from animals.

Often, animals show more evolved behaviour than humans. When you place a sugar cube next to an ant, it will go in search of other ants in the colony so that they can enjoy and profit from it together.

So, until the education system radically changes, we as parents must help children develop awareness of human values. We will have to be the good shepherd, bringing out their innate good character.

Being a good example is again the key. However, many of us have either no time and/or no inclination toward being a good example.

Perhaps we expect school to take care of that character development. But school doesn't – well, most don't – though many manage to do so implicitly and try to do their best.

This brings us to another complicated aspect of parenting – the ongoing discussion as to whether or not the government should intervene in education matters.

I can well understand that, as a parent, you most certainly do not want anyone looking over your shoulder and giving you unwanted advice. I for one believe that the home has its own sanctity and that the government has to stay away from parenting, unless of course there is a threat to the child's life.

However, experience teaches that enhancing your consciousness as a parent through workshops, such as my own *Love and Law Parenting*, has a huge, positive impact on your child. It also has a very positive impact on your parenting, your well-being, and your effectiveness as a parent.

It is time for a change.

# POINTS TO PONDER

*When faced with a choice of*
*schools, take a good look at*
*what the school feels like and*
*find out what its vibe is.*
*Ask yourself if you feel good about*
*the teachers that you see there.*
*Ask a school if they have character*
*building in the curriculum, and*
*if so, how they teach it.*
*Ask them if they value developing*
*the hearts of their students.*
*Does the school teach human values?*
*As for after-school care and day-care*
*places, are all the workers certified,*
*and do they have solid*
*records? Demand to see proof!*
*Your baby/ child depends on it!*
*Only choose day care centres*
*and nurseries that have*
*camera surveillance.*

# CHAPTER 8

## Find Ways to Truly Inspire
## Your Adolescents

Much has been written about puberty. As with all childhoods, puberty is also a culturally defined historical construction. In most of the Western Hemisphere, the period of puberty was considered to take place between the ages of 13 and 19, hence the word teenagers.

In some cultures, it is not unusual for an 11-year-old to become a mother. So it is culture that determines the definition of the teenager or appropriate teen behaviour.

In our part of the world, the age for the onset of puberty has changed. This is due to all kinds of changes in our diet, the tremendous increase of hormones we consume in our food and use for birth control, and small genetic changes. This book has been written with American and European people as a reference point. My philosophy, however, is *one world*, one caste – the caste of humanity!

In Western Europe, a girl in the seventeenth or eighteenth century would have her first period around her 17th year. In 1897 in Holland, for example, girls had their first period around the age of 16. By the end of the nineteenth century, the average age had gone down to 15.

Another leap downwards occurred in the 1950s and 1960s, due mostly to improved standards of living. By 1965, this had dropped to an average of 13.4. By 1980, it was 13.28 years.

The latest statistics speak of an average of 12.5 years; however, it varies from ages 10 to 16. In South America, the average age is 11. Scientists do not expect a further decrease (similar historical data at http://www.mum. org/menarage.htm).

More and more parents have started seeing pubescent behaviour around the ages of 10 to 11. And then many children go on living in the family home till they are 19 or 20 years old – sometimes even well into their 20s. You could say that nowadays, there seems to be a very elongated period of puberty, which runs from ages 10 to 20.

Adolescence is marked by huge challenges and problems. A large number of these issues are determined by hormonal developments. These are not just sexual hormones, but other growth hormones too, as well as changes in the brain. This is a very interesting period where the development of the inner being, as opposed to the development of the sexual hormones, warrants a great deal more attention than it currently receives.

### *Spiritual awareness in adolescence builds a foundation for responsible adulthood.*

Professor Joseph Chilton Pearce, and other scientists, have discovered that there is a part of the brain that, around the ages of 11 or 12, starts to develop a need for spiritual input and development (http://www. goodreads.com/book/show/1708349.Evolution_s_ End). Various esoteric and religious groups have always emphasized that manifesting our innate divine nature is the reason for our being, and hence, needs serious consideration and care.

Modern society and modern media have, on the one hand, enabled us to gain access to all these teachings worldwide; yet at the same time, they are corrupting and degrading humanity to bestial levels. Just as the pubescent need for spiritual sustenance begins to develop, our current culture starts to fill the brain's need for meaning with...

- pop stars (the word *stars* is a prime example of a world turned upside down: real stars in the skies are mostly ignored, singers and actors are elevated to that status for no good reason at all, and real constellations have been reduced to car names – Subaru being the Japanese word for the Pleiades – not to mention the cars bearing the names of Greek gods)
- movie stars (also often bad role models)
- (generally) very boring education
- widespread pornography and violence through movies, games, the Internet, and mobile phones
- greed encouraged by commercials and music channels

These are definitely not accommodating an evolutionary need! In fact, the exact opposite is achieved. In this crucial period, there is an enormous need/ emptiness in the brain and in the soul that is fed with emotions and great negativity. It results in adoration of unattainable idols that usually lead a life without boundaries, commercialism that promises happiness that can only be purchased, and so on.

Recent articles show us that many shootings and other violent acts by teenagers have been inspired by their favourite movies and games. Teenage killers frequently tell police investigators they were inspired by video games. Furthermore, research has finally confirmed that watching TV at the ages of one to three leads to sleeplessness, learning disorders, depression, aggression, and nightmares! (http:// health.howstuffworks.com/ pregnancy-and-parenting/baby-health/ infant-health/ baby-tv.htm).

Keep in mind that you need to critically read all the research in this area. Research about the effects of modern media attracts no interest. The ones that are in favour are almost always to be linked to either a paying client in the business or some source with a link to vested interests.

If as parents we want to ensure that our children are *truly fed* in early puberty, we will need to actively deal with the question, *in what manner can I give my child a foundation of spirituality or morality?* This actually applies to all parents, whether you are an atheist or a believer, spiritual or highly religious. By just being aware of this fact, you will be able to make a highly valuable contribution to the well- being of your teenager, and even more so to his or her development.

Furthermore, it is a given that when parents and educators actively contribute to this spiritual development, the children then flourish in all areas. School performance increases. Behaviour at home and at school improves dramatically. These teens use less drugs and alcohol, have fewer problems with violence, are more sociable, have a bigger network, and so on. At a later age, these teenagers (by now, adults) have fewer problems, better career options, are in better health, have less encounters with the law, and have better relationships.

And yet, notwithstanding your best intentions as a parent to give your children or teenagers all good things, their development can go awry much more often than we would like it to. That is due to the fact that all the previously mentioned negative influences are very strong and very well organized. Children are brainwashed 24x7 with commercials that contribute little or nothing to their happiness and moral development.

For some people, *moral development* has an unpleasant ring to it. In Oops! The Parenting Handbook, moral development is seen as something very positive that all parents wish their children to develop. It enables you to have the necessary discernment to ask yourself, before you make a choice, whether your action is good or bad, whether your deed will have a positive or a negative outcome.

### *Find fun structured ways to provide children the meaning they seek.*

You, as a parent, must first become aware of the process of successfully countering the previously mentioned negative influences on our children's lives. Next, you must consider in what structured and attractive manner you can supply your children with fun and inspiring input to give form to their need for meaning. Courses on this subject are available through the author or at www.loveandlaw.nl and at www.oopstheparentinghandbook.com

Some teenagers seem to gain a degree of inspiration from existing religions; others find inspiration or satisfaction with various spiritual schools, academic institutions, or enlightened teachers.

However, the large majority are not offered anything whatsoever that will fulfil their natural need for spiritual growth, for actual evolution. As soon as you as a parent are aware of this need, you can start to make your child conscious of it, too. For instance, you can make sure that you offer them a course or enrol them at a library or offer them a journey that is filled with inspiring aspects. And I do not have malls and gaming establishments in mind.

You can engage your child in an open dialogue on the matter and discuss what aspects played a part in your own moral and spiritual development or the lack of it.

### Talk about sex.

In this chapter on hormones, it is, of course, also necessary to discuss sexuality.

When the subject of sex was discussed, a 17-year-old client of mine said, 'She and I, we don't use the word sex but feel that we make love.' This is endearing, wonderful, and so true.

All too often, the media reduces *making love* to *sex, the F word,* and so on. *Making love* is a nice alternative, whereas teenagers also go with *making out, doing it,* and so on. In addition, women are portrayed mostly as objects, and terribly derogatory terminology is used. The whole discussion of *sex* versus *making love* is one that we will not get into here.

What is important, however, is that teenagers are also inundated with sexually oriented information. An overload of pornography on the Internet, in magazines and movies, through downloads on cell phones, and in many music clips all using sex as a marketing tool. And all of these seem to convey the message: *It is perfectly normal, nothing is weird, and do whatever you like.*

Unfortunately, this message gets further distorted in a growing number of children who use sex as a trading commodity for all kinds of transactions – and sex was not intended for that.

## Use discussion to expose and eradicate double standards in gender relations.

Of course, there is a refreshing core of truth when you tell children or teenagers that sex is natural and healthy. And it is even more so when you set it off against old-fashioned and wrong judgments of sex being sinful, et cetera. Sex (making love) can be very normal, healthy, fun, and highly fulfilling.

But there is more to it. At the age of their first sexual experiences, teenagers are extremely vulnerable. Often, their sense of self-worth is determined by their sex life or lack of it.

On the one hand, the media and society insist that sex is good, necessary, and cool... and not only sex, but also dressing and acting like an available sex object. On the other hand, a woman will most often be judged and condemned if she does these things. A woman with many partners is still considered 'loose', a 'tramp', and so on. Because there are double standards, a man is considered cool and masculine in the same situation.

## Understand the dangers intimacy poses.

When two young people have sexual relations, there is often a huge degree of intimacy and vulnerability. When things are problematic at home or at school, a sexual relationship will often offer an apparent solution for all problems. It is of the utmost importance that, as a parent, we talk to our children about human sexuality, or that we at least show them where to find neutral educational resources about sexuality.

Research tells us that, despite 30 years of sexual education in the West, many taboos still prevail. This can only be because of the way we relate to sexuality at home. It is not at all strange that you as a parent should do as much as possible to make sex a topic of discussion, if only to make your daughter and son aware of the several dangerous aspects of indiscriminate sex and the so-called highly criminal and organized 'lover boys'.

We need to be positive and empowering with our children, but at the same time, we need to tell them about the horrifying fact that there is a huge criminal business out there that spends all its time and considerable resources looking to kidnap babies, children, and teenagers to sell as sex slaves. With teenagers, they usually pose as interested lovers and start to shower their object of affection with gifts. Then at an unexpected moment, they make them leave their homes or just kidnap the unsuspecting victims.

Parental guidance and monitoring are very important in these matters. It is not so much the biological aspect of sex that needs discussing, as there is more than enough information available about the physical act; it is the emotional and psychological facets that need attention. And it needs to be stressed that sex is natural and that the erogenous zones of our bodies are beautiful and natural.

Experience teaches us that engaging our children in a dialogue on the above topics has many good results. The extent of openness, understanding, and respect determine the quality and level of the communication. This is based on feedback from parents over more than 17 years of experience in my parenting practice, as well as what therapist and psychologist colleagues report.

## *Counteract the media's terrible influence on body image.*

Insecurity about their own puberty, in part due to the completely out-of-control cosmetic industry, is so vast that a recent Dutch survey tells us that eight out of 10 youngsters are dissatisfied about their own bodies and would consider cosmetic surgery (http:// www.proud2bme.nl/ Artikelen_over_gezondheid/80_ procent_van_10_jarigen_op_dieet).

Cosmetic operations by teenagers have increased from 1997 to 2007 by 475 per cent! Approximately 75 per cent of teen girls feel depressed, guilty, and ashamed after reading women's magazines. More than 80 per cent of 10-year-olds have been on a diet at least once, and 78 per cent of 17-year-olds are dissatisfied with their own bodies.

At the time of printing the international edition of Oops! the first catalogue for underwear ('bodywear') for children of ages four to 12 was released, and it included bras, thongs, and garters. For four to 12-year-olds? If there is a single reader who can explain to me why there is nothing wrong with this, I would like to hear from you. Meanwhile, there was such a public outcry that the company withdrew the catalogue and the items.

A large group of youth, aged 10 and older, who are dissatisfied about their own looks, are being guided by misleading images that are almost always digitally enhanced. Those images make teenagers even more insecure about their own bodies than they already were.

# POINTS TO PONDER

*How do you view sexuality? Your bodies?*
*What do you want to pass on to your children?*
   *Are you relaxed when discussing sex?*
*How will you buffer the mad onslaught of*
   *sex and pornography in the media?*
*Does your PC have Internet filters and blocks?*
*Check all chat histories and websites your*
   *children have been on. Experience teaches*
   *us that you cannot be careful enough.*
*Make children aware of the serious*
   *possible consequences of unprotected*
   *sex, including STDs and pregnancy.*
*As soon as puberty sets in, respect the sexuality*
   *of your child/teenager. Be discreet about*
   *your own nudity as well as theirs but be*
   *natural when discussing the body.*
*Humour goes hand in hand with sex; do not*
   *be too serious about it.*
*If you need a good warning, the movie The Captive*
   *(2014) and the Liam Neeson movie* Taken *–*
   *specifically the first one are good but frightening*
   *sources of the highly organized business of child*
   *abduction– and watch it with your*
   *teenagers.*
*Read online about the horrifying statistics of*
   *the worldwide sex slave trade.*

# ACTION PLAN

---
---
---
---
---
---
---
---
---
---
---
---
---
---
---
---
---
---
---
---
---
---
---

# CHAPTER 9

# Alcohol and Drugs

We often hear large number of children/teenagers showing up at the Emergency Room (ER) with enormous amounts of alcohol in their blood. An alcohol percentage that is equal to the intake of *1.3 gallons* of Breezers (an alcoholic beverage that tastes like a soft drink) is not an exception! That is a lot of little bottles. These are, of course, excesses. And then people will make haste to say that every generation worries about the licentious behaviour of teenagers. However, when you look at the statistics, there is a huge problem. There is a steady yet sharp increase of alcohol and drug abuse. The average age that children turn to drinking and drugs is steadily decreasing.

By drugs, I mean the smoking of marijuana and hash and the taking of ecstasy, LSD, GHB, mescaline, crystal meth, crack, poppers, magic mushrooms, cocaine, heroin, morphine, Quaaludes, and so on.

There is a large group of middle and upper-class parents that is convinced that substance abuse will never enter their *proper neighbourhoods* or their *proper schools*. However, sadly, substance abuse knows no boundaries. Whatever your belief or attitude may be, it is of the utmost importance to put this issue on the agenda in your communities. I believe it is important to realize that several aspects play a role here:

1.  The commercial availability and marketing of intoxicants: Alcohol (and to some extent drugs and smoking) are still seen as *cool* by many children and teenagers. Commercials always show happy, popular people drinking and smoking. A party is not considered to be a party unless alcohol is included. In many countries, liquor is even available at petrol stations and from a wide array of 24-hour shops. The most ruthless *marketing* machines worldwide are those of the drug cartels, liquor and cigarette manufacturers, as well as pharmaceutical companies. Obviously drug cartels do not do traditional marketing, but they employ ruthless strategies to get as many people as possible hooked on their product.

2.  The history of alcohol and drugs, as well as cultural aspects: For the last few hundred years, drugs and alcohol have been big business. These intoxicants have been fought over and prohibited in various forms at various times. In many so-called *primitive societies*, drugs, and to a lesser extent alcohol, are only taken during special ceremonies and celebrations, thus having a clear communal purpose. The only societies that I believe are primitive are many of our current Western societies that have been fighting thousands of wars over the last five thousand years, and are doing everything they can to eradicate as many species as possible, while destroying our environment, not to mention the killing and torturing of millions in the name of their God by, for instance, the Catholic Church. The so-called *primitive* societies tend to have a huge respect for – and understanding of – Mother Nature. In *modern* culture, drinking is a social norm, in the sense that almost every gathering from family dinners to any event with friends includes alcohol. An exception would be most Hindu and all Muslim gatherings/ people.

There is a ruthless marketing machine out there with only one goal – to make sure as many youths start drinking as early as possible! The mainstream media do not help when they sometimes state that *there is no real youth alcohol problem*, and that *every previous generation was binge drinking as well.*

What is not taken into account is the fact that the starting age for drinking has decreased dramatically over the last two decades, as well as the fact that the types of alcohol and their content has also changed. Mixers are packaged to look identical to non alcoholic beverages, and they contain even more sugars and dyes. They are an innocuous-looking entry for children into the world of alcohol.

Regarding drugs, almost every school in the Western Hemisphere has its own drug dealers who deal both within the school as well as on the playground. And yes, this includes that perfect, expensive private school your child is attending. Furthermore, pop and rock idols tend to make drug abuse glamorous and cool. Nothing could be further from the truth, and the drug related suicides are a yearly occurrence in and around Hollywood. Many of these users end up in and out of rehab because, contrary to popular belief, drugs are in charge, not you. Look at any tabloid.

## Many cultures used alcohol and drugs as part of initiation rites or healing.

People are quick to add that children in most European countries also start drinking at an early age. True, but that is usually a glass of very diluted wine, and more importantly, it takes place under adult supervision.

Throughout history, there have been a few cultures where the use of drugs plays a role in certain initiation rites. In these cultures, drugs are used by the medicine men and healers for growth and healing. This implies a well-prepared event full of meaning that actually benefits the community. This is dramatically different from how Western cultures use drugs.

From the 1960s up to today, drugs are considered to be a portal to another level of consciousness and inner growth, but one that unfortunately causes one to linger there, thus beginning a dependence that becomes difficult to shake off. There are, however, other ways of developing your consciousness such as through meditation. More often than not, drugs are escape valves. In this case, you are reduced to your own hedonism, and/or to knock yourself out. In the West, many cannot even relax without a joint. Again some people may benefit from "soft" drugs but there is a fine line between use and abuse and it takes a strong non addictive personality to be able to guard that boundary.

Interestingly enough, there is much less drug abuse in the East than in the West. Perhaps one reason for that could be the fact that in many Asian cultures they tend to place less emphasis on the intellect and more on a rich spiritual heritage. There is nothing wrong with social drinking, it can be relaxing, and highly enjoyable.

## Powerful drug cartels can be defeated by responsible personal choices.

Worldwide drug cartels are very well-organized international conglomerates whose goals are turnover, profit, and worldwide domination! Be aware that the government, law enforcement agencies, the society as a whole are not undertaking any substantial effort to stop the drug trade – even worse, we uphold it. If these parties really wanted to stop the drug trade, they would have, as they have enough power and tools to do so.

This is also the case with the pharmaceutical industry and the alcohol and drug industries. They hold enormous clout, and thus are able to spread their poison. This does not include essential medicines, and it does not include the casual pleasure of a glass of wine, beer, or champagne. Nothing is wrong with that as long as we can also apply the age-old adage of moderation being key, an important point for parents to teach their children (by good example).

## Parents play a crucial role in protecting children from the threat of drugs.

Parents have various ways of coping: some are terrified of the idea that their children will come into contact with drugs; other parents are very tolerant. In this difficult context, how can we as parents be effective in our preventative measures regarding drugs?

First of all, we must *acknowledge* this threat. Though many schools do their best to address the issue, we, too, need to take responsibility as parents. We must recognize the need to discuss the dangers with your children and teenagers.

Secondly, we must *offer attractive alternatives.* The appeal of drugs can be very strong, and the only option is to offer an equally appealing alternative. Depending on the circumstances, that alternative may be sports, a hobby, or spiritual growth/consciousness, giving your child or teenager enough self-knowledge and self-satisfaction to prevent the search for anything outside of himself or herself. When there is no growth in the areas of inner growth and spiritual fulfilment, the child or teenager tends to become much more vulnerable to addiction and/or substance abuse! Other options may be yoga, meditation, the creative arts, music, kung fu, and so on.

Your children will soon discover that true happiness and bliss is their own true nature – not a result of substance dependency – and that true happiness is always within their reach.

# POINTS TO PONDER

*Discuss with your partner/friend how you
    view drugs and alcohol.*

*What attitudes do you wish to pass on to
    your children?*

*In your given environment, what will
    and won't your teenagers be exposed
    to or be able to indulge in?*

*Check out online the tell-tale signals of drug
    usage. When in doubt, don't be afraid to
    purchase a urine test. This is not cool, I know,
    but an addicted child is totally uncool, right?*

*Offer attractive alternatives.*

*How can you be loving and give love?
    This cannot be emphasized enough.
    Most addictions stem from a lack of
    love! Fight addiction with building
    self-confidence, good company/peer pressure,
    and coping mechanisms.*

*How can you help your child to evolve
    into a loving human being? This will
    reduce the need for external stimuli.*

*Watch out for boredom. This means
    the door to external thrills and
    temptations is wide open.*

*Stay alert! Educate and update
    yourself on the latest data.*

*One last cliché – make sure they do
    plenty of sports.*

# ACTION PLAN

_____

_____

_____

_____

_____

_____

_____

_____

_____

_____

_____

_____

_____

_____

_____

_____

_____

_____

_____

_____

_____

# CHAPTER 10

## College

There are advantages to academic pursuit. It teaches young adults to think, their intellect develops, and their talents flourish. The pursuit of a degree is, however, all too often driven by the hunger for status, profit, and fame. Many people will study in order to become someone who is *great* rather than someone who is *good*.

Based upon my extensive experience with parents, teenagers, school, and education in general, we can benefit tremendously from spending time thinking about all the ins and outs of education and life goals prior to making choices regarding study and direction in life. All too often, these choices are made based upon quick decisions, general ideas, parental influence, societal pressure, and what is deemed useful or popular or financially sound. Please consider letting your deliberations include aspects, such as human values, becoming fulfilled in life, and contributing to society and our planet.

Good education ought to prepare you for life and not only enable you – as it presently does – to go out and beg for a job. 'Education is not merely for earning a living, but should be for learning how to live' (http:// www.sssbpt.info/sssspeaks/volume24/sss24-27.pdf).

Our society is regularly shaken up by corruption scandals – corrupt royalty, corrupt politicians, corrupt public servants, corrupt businessmen, corrupt policemen, and so on. What do you expect? When schools and universities fail to teach you about human values and about spiritual development, then you will not develop a sense of what is good and bad.

Thus, there are no brakes on your greed, and you have no qualms about abusing your position and power. When your education teaches you about human values and how to apply them, you learn to listen to your heart and conscience. This, in turn, makes you a professional equipped with those beautiful qualities that make you a good and decent human being!

There are plenty of people who want to become great, yet few who strive for goodness. We are inundated worldwide by examples of people who have struck gold. There are millions of millionaires and billionaires all over the world. Has this put an end to all the hunger and starvation in the world? Are there fewer wars? No, on the contrary, there is more dissatisfaction, hate, and violence than ever before.

The wealthy ought to share more of their wealth. More importantly, at an early age, we need to learn to develop our innate good human qualities as well as our moral sense, which has nothing whatsoever to do with organized religion. We need a new generation of graduates who are ready to share their talents with their fellow human beings. These will be people who develop academically and professionally, but who tend equally to their humanity. Only then will the world change. So as a parent, there is an important task ahead of you...

## *Seek colleges that foster applying human values.*

Firstly, choose a school or college (or help your children to do so) that pays attention to and applies human values to as many aspects of their curriculum as possible.

As a parent, you can help your children develop their own inner moral compass and compassion. One way to do this is to ask them before they undertake an action what the effect will be. Will it have a positive, negative, or neutral outcome? Such as: *If the CEO and CFO of Enron would have done this, they might be lounging at home instead of in prison?*

Generally speaking, the education field has been divided in two: schools geared only toward academic growth and schools geared toward academic growth from a religious background.

## *Help keep moral compasses intact*

Perhaps as parents (as voters, and as stakeholders in education), we can encourage our educational institutions to start applying comprehensive explicit human values. Many colleges and universities that are inspired by a religion tend to limit the teaching of human values to their religious views or the ancient teachers that their institutes are based on. What we need now are schools and colleges that teach human values and timeless truths in a modern manner, free from religious dogma or propaganda.

Training to all staff throughout all aspects of the curriculum is necessary. This is not very complicated; it merely requires the will to do so and include the topic in all academic discussions, both among staff as well as students. We as parents have so much more power than we realize to influence our educational institutes. If a few million parents raise the issue of human values a few times, that in itself will lead to discussions about the necessity of the topic.

The consistent application of human values throughout the curriculum will lead to a new generation of academicians who have developed both their brains and their hearts.

## *Be aware that college isn't always the only or best option.*

Related to our discussion on studying, there are a few other important matters to consider.

- The time when a degree was a ticket to a job is long gone. For instance, as I write this, youth unemployment is up to a staggering 50 per cent in some European countries. In India, annually 500,000 college graduates are unemployed the second they graduate. In the United States, nearly 1.5 million 17- to 24-year-olds are unemployed. (http://www.huffingtonpost. com/2013/05/20/ america-youth-unemployment_n_3306089. html).

- You can develop yourself without a college degree.
- Academic knowledge does not lead to self-knowledge or knowledge of people.
- By keeping as many young people as possible in college, government/society keeps them out of mainstream society (to some degree). They are taught to listen and to be as docile as possible, as well as to be good consumers.
- This in turn enables you to pacify them in the corporate world and society in general.
- This turns them into complacent, dependent, and often fearful, well-behaved consumers.
- Most colleges and universities do not teach you to think critically and independently. They teach you to think the way they want you to think. A huge difference.

So, before you advise your child to go to college, at least be critical about your choice of college. Do not expect school or college to supply your children with self-knowledge, and do not expect them to be educated in the most important human values either. That is something you, as their parents, will need to teach them. It goes without saying that I am generalizing. Of course, there are wonderful teachers out there who are extremely inspirational. And yes, there are many schools and colleges out there that offer more than knowledge alone. It is up to us to seek them out.

### *Avoid hindering young adults by making them afraid.*

In our love for our children, invariably fear enters into the equation. We love them, adore them, and worship them. Mothers carry them in their wombs and then suckle them at their breasts. It is natural that, at times, we are afraid for their well-being.

When it comes to the future, choice of school, college, and life path, fear tends to enter into our decisions. It often unconsciously sneaks its way into our reasoning and into our advice. And that is not a good place to be. So, please let us be aware of what kinds of emotions we let seep into our communication with our children. Let us realize the importance of basing our advice and comments on our faith, trust, and belief in our children, in our teenagers! Let us have firm faith that we have equipped them with all that they will need to succeed in life. Let us manifest and speak our belief in them and their potential.

Throughout history, change has been a constant. All too often, we tend to advise our children against certain choices with statements about how that vocation does not make one wealthy, how certain studies are not commercially sound, and so on. This is not right. We need to respect the choices our children and teenagers make, because, barring extreme cases of delinquency, their intuition and inner guidance tend to be much purer than our own!

What we can do is listen to them, and together with them analyse and try to feel how a certain choice would unfold and what the pros and cons of that choice could be. However, keeping in mind that nobody can predict the future or the outcome of their choices; they will learn from bearing the consequences of their choices, which leads to growth and development and wisdom!

# POINTS TO PONDER

*Encourage your children's dreams.
Guide them, but let them decide
what is good for them.*

*Stop making your child afraid:
'With that degree you will never
earn a living', and so on.*

*Unconditionally express your complete
faith in your child! The mother of
well-known actress Charlize Theron
gave her a one-way (!) ticket to Los
Angeles. This is complete and utter
faith in your child! And it worked!*

*Coach your child/teenager when they
are undecided. Gather information
regarding their studies, career
path, and profession.*

# ACTION PLAN

_____

_____

_____

_____

_____

_____

_____

_____

_____

_____

_____

_____

_____

_____

_____

_____

_____

_____

_____

_____

# CHAPTER 11

## Leaving Home Can be Good
## for Both Parent and Child

Leaving home at 18 is no longer a natural step.

It is said that puberty stretches from 11 to 28 these days, meaning that teenagers remain dependent on their parents in all kinds of ways. Even though they might go to college, many still live at home as well. Many teenagers who do not go to college and start looking for work, live at home for financial and/or cultural reasons.

Your role as a parent changes with every age group. During the first years, you are a full-time caretaker. After a while, your role changes to a more advisory function in addition to the caretaking. In puberty, roles need to be redefined. As parents, your role becomes more like that of a coach. You start to stand *next* to your child instead of *above* your child.

In this phase, it is important that you start to prepare your child for the inevitability of adulthood and independence.

Mothers in particular have a very hard time letting go of their sons and daughters, and as mothers and fathers, you need to learn to let go. For example, the possibility of your child joining the armed forces and realizing that, at the age of 18, he or she is legally licensed to kill can be very hard on a parent. I know letting go is easier said than done; yet, you need to do so. Furthermore, all kinds of rights are attained, including voting and the right to drive a car (which sometimes happens at an even younger age). Yet often, we treat our 16, 17, or 18-year-olds like little children.

Generally, teens live at home with their parents. Thus, they enjoy all the benefits with few or no responsibilities. They are fed, and financially, they are completely taken care of and catered to. Their tendency is to run to a parent for help for anything they need.

## Provide rites of passage to welcome teens to adulthood.

Intelligent cultures mark puberty as the onset of adulthood. After whatever rites of passage the teens have gone through, they are treated as adults and given equal status and rights as well as added responsibilities!

This is something most Western *"civilized cultures"* fail to pay any attention to. So we create a more and more rebellious and immature generation of youngsters. Much vandalism is the result of a cry for attention that could be avoided if these boys and girls were given significant societal rites. Very often, youth delinquency is an attractive alternative, due to its abundant rituals, attention, and bonds. They give youngsters the feeling that their lives matter, that they have something to contribute.

The question is, as parents, *how can we provide rites of passage in our children's lives?*

The best place to start is in your community. Sit down with other parents whom you know and find kindred spirits open to the idea of providing rites of passage. Some examples that come to mind are provided here.

Make a nature trip and think of some creative challenges and rituals that mark their entrance into adulthood. Perhaps you can sit down with your teens and ask them what they would like to do. Community projects are another option that can give a group of teens a huge boost. Girls and mothers could use the onset of the first menstruation as a moment to engage in a meaningful ritual together. The possibilities are endless.

Also, you can help them by engaging in open, fruitful dialogues about their views on society. Using quotes can be a great way to start these discussions. Since teens can tend to be rebellious or question society, it can be useful to use that premise as a starting point. Ultimately, this will help them realize that it is our planet, that humanity is one, and that we need to share and lose our selfishness in order to thrive and survive.

> *It is no measure of health to be well adjusted to a profoundly sick society*
> J. Krishnamurti

Furthermore, hard physical work/sports are necessary to avoid getting into trouble. It is a matter of energy distribution. Teens often have too much bottled-up energy. Providing outlets such as sports, singing, drama, and charity and community work rituals allows the energy to be channelled into positive outlets. In youngsters who do not feel that they can contribute to positive influences such as society, culture, and environment, the energy comes out differently: violently and destructively.

Taking all of the above into account, what can we do as parents? How do we optimally prepare our children for the great move away from home?

- Give them self-confidence.
- Teach them independent thinking.
- Teach them to be financially self-sufficient.
- Enable them to develop self-knowledge.
- Teach them to listen to their heart and their conscience.
- Be a good example!
- Love them no matter how unsympathetic their behaviour might be to you; love them for who they are

## *Ensure that children leave in harmony.*

There are three main points that I would like to address.

1. This can be a difficult time for parents, as we've devoted our lives to being a parent (empty-nest syndrome).
2. This is also a time when as parents, we can and should grasp new opportunities, both within and outside of the workforce.
3. Parenthood deserves gratitude and recognition that our society doesn't give it. When a child leaves home, as parents, we don't receive the awards and honours due us. We need to change the way society thinks about parenthood, and as parents, we need to honour ourselves and each other.

The period of leaving home has lots of consequences for you as a parent. Specifically for the parent who has been at home most of the time – generally speaking, the mother – this can be a tough time.

### *Celebrating the parenting years and marking the occasion of your child's leaving will help you, the parent, move on more happily with your own life.*

During this period, you need to reconsider your role and who you are. Your being was, after all, determined by your motherhood. The above is much less applicable in the case of the working mother, be it part-time or full-time. For those mothers who do derive a major part of their identity from motherhood, this can be a very difficult period (the so-called empty-nest syndrome).

What now? Often, you discover that, as a mom/ parent, you have given so much of yourself that a feeling of emptiness can follow. For 10 to 20 years, you have given it all: your love, your time, your attention, your money, and your energy. And all of a sudden, they are gone.

When that parting takes place in harmony, the difficulties of this new period are much less significant than when the parting takes place with conflicts. This is another reason why it is important that children leave in harmony.

The patterns that we establish at key points in life, such as this one, are crucial determinants of our future lives. Disharmony at moments like this can and will often lead to a lifetime of disharmonious patterns, and so positive patterns at home will lead to a possible lifetime of positive ones. You can compare these dynamics to the statistics that show us that children of divorced parents are two to three times more likely themselves to be divorced later on in life (http://www.divorce.usu. edu/ files/uploads/Lesson5.pdf).

Generally, the main caretaker is okay career-wise; however, many women who have given up their career opportunities to be a full-time or part-time mom discover the loss. Regrettably, our society does not value motherhood as it ought to. As I have stated at the beginning of this book, the quality of our parenting determines the future of our country.

Therefore, we owe all our parents an infinite debt of gratitude, and the mothers deserve most of that grateful recognition.

However, in stark contrast with the corporate world where recognition, perks, and bonuses are awarded for dedication and services, there is hardly any acknowledgment of the effort and the tremendous sacrifice that have been made in the course of parenting. No bonus, no title, no media write-up, no golden parachute, et cetera.

And that should change.

When children leave home, it should be celebrated with prizes, speeches, a fun vacation, or some other significant gift.

This also marks this period/event positively. This period has another positive side for the parent who took care of the largest part of the upbringing: you are now able to focus on developing yourself – with the added advantage that you are older and hopefully wiser.

The Internet offers unlimited possibilities for undertaking ventures from the home or wherever you are. Furthermore, thanks to the Internet, while being a parent or when active parenting has finished, there are plenty of opportunities for self-development and/or education. This fits in perfectly with the trend and government plans to have people remain in the workforce longer.

Wisdom does indeed often come with the years, and when you have fared well throughout your parenting years, you have a treasure trove of experience. As a domestic manager, you have as much experience and knowledge related to managing a challenging group as does many a manager in the corporate world! And often, this has taken place under very strenuous circumstances: irregular hours, sickness, and other stress factors.

You're catching my drift by now, I assume. I believe that, as a parent, you should be proud of your achievements. You can be happy and grateful for what you are doing, and I feel that our society needs to show much more respect for and appreciation of parenting!

You might ask, *what does this have to with leaving home?* Everything!

At the point where you as a parent reintegrate into the workforce, the years of *investment* in your parenting should be an extremely valued asset on your résumé! Corporations and institutions should be thrilled to have you as a possible candidate. At present, it is an upside-down world due to the intolerable arrogance of the male-dominated corporate world. But times are changing!

Not only that, but also at all those parties, dinners, and social functions where a parent (generally the woman) shares that she takes care of the children, the conversation quickly ends or the subject is changed, often leaving the woman in question with feelings of unworthiness. In fact, we should be happy that a domestic manager is present in our circle, and we should see what we can learn from her. In order for that to happen, it is necessary for us all to be more conscious of this aspect.

Another related problem is the exaggerated adulation of money and power. Parenting has little to add to that. You are easily *cool* in a group when it is all about your newest product, your recent captivating management meeting, or the latest corporate merger. But the managing of the home, the baby's first steps and words, and the conflict with the day-care centre have little allure.

Let us all make sure that parenting regains the status and recognition that it deserves.

# POINTS TO PONDER

*Do you believe rites of passage*
*are important?*
*Will they be of significance for you and*
*your partner to help your child*
*transition to adulthood?*
*Would it be helpful for you to provide*
*rites of passage for your teenager?*
*Research with your child the different*
*traditional rites of passage in*
*various cultures of the world.*
*How can you empower your*
*child to make confident*
*academic and career choices?*
*In what way can you make*
*the transition of leaving*
*home harmonious?*
*How can you as a parent*
*empower yourself after your*
*children leave home?*

# ACTION PLAN

_____

_____

_____

_____

_____

_____

_____

_____

_____

_____

_____

_____

_____

_____

_____

_____

_____

_____

_____

_____

_____

_____

# CHAPTER 12

# Parenting Styles:
# The Importance of Authoritative Parenting

'And they lived happily ever after...'

Thus all fairy tales end, and it is a fitting finale to the essence of your life as a parent.

Almost all parents want their children to be happy. They want them to have good jobs, develop themselves, have nice friends, make lots of money, have a nice partner, et cetera. Often, it all comes into being as you had hoped that it would.

All too often, however, these good wishes are surpassed by all sorts of other unfavourable developments: problems at home, problems at school, strife, sadness, health problems, and later on problems with alcohol, drugs, sex, criminal behaviour, et cetera. No parent would wish for any of these problems for his or her child.

So why does it all too often end up going that way? My own extensive experience, as well as that of many colleagues worldwide, shows us that there is one parenting style that is very effective.

*This is called authoritative parenting.*

There are two more main styles: authoritarian parenting and permissive parenting. Research and experience show us that the last two parenting styles have many negative consequences.

The following is a summary of the three parenting styles and the qualities they bring about in children.

## Authoritative

- The parents are equal partners.
- They make mutual decisions.
- The children are consulted.
- Parents are experienced as being fair and reasonable.
- It leads to the following qualities and characteristics in children: honesty, integrity, caution, articulate, trusting, courageous, emotionally strong, exhibiting inner guidance, freedom, discipline, resistance to peer pressure

## Permissive

- Parents are too busy.
- Children are not consulted.
- It leads to the following qualities and characteristics in children: dependence, outward orientation, low competency, complaining, blaming, critical, low self-esteem, low self-confidence, indiscipline, impulsiveness

## Authoritarian

- The parents use threats.
- The children are exploited.
- Hypocrisy is evident.

- It leads to the following qualities and characteristics in children: self-doubt, avoidance, low self-esteem, lying, violent behaviour, bullying, verbal violence, insecurity, aggression/anger

This overview leaves no doubt: authoritative parenting is the ideal parenting style. It is an ideal mix of rules and freedom, and a balance between parental authority and input from the child.

## *Reflect upon your parenting style, and if needed, have the courage to make a change.*

There are plenty of examples of children and even of whole generations that have been raised by authoritarian and/or permissive parenting. They illustrate all too well what the far-reaching consequences of parenting are.

Take, for instance, the emotional trauma of so many of the previous generations that were raised by strict parents who would spare no physical abuse. Or the often weak-willed and misguided results of children raised by permissive *laissez-faire* parents who thought everything was okay and who said *no* to nothing.

These two parenting styles regretfully lead to all kinds of undesirable behaviour, and even to undesirable personalities.

In reaction to the often too-strict parenting of the last centuries, many parents of the last 40 years or so turned to a too permissive style of parenting.

For instance, when researching criminals and how they were brought up, in almost all cases, there were one or more authoritarian parents or parental figures. Among many drug addicts, the parents or parental figures were often found to be very permissive and/or violent at times.

Many parents still believe that permissive parenting has no drawbacks. They couldn't be more wrong (http:// www.fountainmagazine.com/ Issue/detail/Parenting-Styles-How-They-Affect-Children). Research and experience show us that permissive parenting leads to many serious problems, and therefore yields unhappy children and adults.

Authoritative parenting leads to children with those qualities that almost all parents wish to see. These are honest, virtuous children who are full of self-confidence and who trust their inner prompting and follow their hearts. They are open children who know how to find a good balance between spontaneity, enjoying themselves freely and openly, and being fun and respectful with other children, while respecting their integrity.

As parents, if we wish to bring our parenting to a happy end, we will need to seriously think about the above-mentioned aspects of parenting. We will need to ask ourselves, *will my parenting result in what I wish to see in my child*? This implies that we will need to evaluate our parenting styles honestly and critically in order to determine if they are effective.

### *Be willing to consider that the partner you have problems with may still be a good parent for your child.*

Furthermore, it is of the utmost importance that parents agree about their parenting methods! In the case of divorced parents, this is even more important. Regrettably, most parents end up fighting over the children well after the divorce is a fact. I cannot count the number of intelligent, kind mothers I have seen in my practice who would all swear as to how they would do anything to benefit their child. They would agree wholeheartedly when I asked them if they had the consideration of the children above all else.

Then, when arose the issue of custody or allocating time for the father to spend with his children, they would turn like a leaf in the wind and declare solemnly their reasons for not allowing the father custody or for allowing him as little time as possible with his children. All of a sudden, they were even willing to renege on their previous adamant statements on the prime importance of the child's well-being.

I had quite a hard time getting these mothers to realize the folly of their tactics... because ultimately, there is only *one* thing that matters to the child and that is in his or her best interest – time with both parents! So, even if the other parent is a *"loser"* of some kind by society standards, as long as he or she does no harm to the children, then that parent has equal right to spend time with them.

I am obviously stretching the point here, but the exaggeration can be excused in light of the paramount importance of highlighting how heart-breaking it is to see parents fighting out their frustrations over divorce behind their children's backs.

When you do agree on your parenting styles as parents, there is always room for individual differences. And of course, there are differences between men and women in their roles as parents, and that is fine.

Obviously, in the case of new partners and/or stepchildren, it is only natural that there will be completely divergent approaches. Then it is crucial to sit down and discuss common goals.

As a parent, you will need to keep developing your consciousness in all that you do as well as in your motives. Take a good look at the information above on the three parenting styles. As a parent-to-be, you can evaluate what kind of behaviour or traits you would like your children to have, and then gear your parenting towards that goal.

On the other hand, you can also observe the behaviour of your children and then relate it to the following action plan.

- Practice what you preach, setting a good example above all else.
- Remember the two main pillars of successful parenting: *love* and *law*. Then your parenting will most definitely result in all the good things that you wish to develop in your children.
- Be kind to yourself and keep breathing.

# POINTS TO PONDER

*Observe your children's behaviour
carefully. Do you see behaviour that
can be found in the list of permissive
or authoritarian parenting? Then
it might be time to do
things differently.*

*Check the qualities in both lists. How
strict is strict for you and your
child? What can you do and when
should you do it before one type of
behaviour from one list becomes
something worse from another list?*

*Evaluate your own upbringing/
childhood. What style of parenting
did your parents and educators
apply? How has this influenced
your own parenting style? What
would you like to retain? What
would you like to change?*

*Do your children model qualities/
characteristics from the list
of authoritative parenting?
Congratulations! Celebrate life
and each other!*

# Conclusion

I wish you lots of success and fun with your further parenting! I have written Oops! I wish I had known this before, The Parenting Handbook with a heart full of love.

In the more than 15 years of experience in my own parenting practice, as well as during my career in the fields of education and social health services, I have seen, regrettably all too often, the highly disturbing consequences of bad parenting and negative parenting. Even then, there was a lot that we were able to correct and heal, but more often than not, this happened too late.

If my words sound harsh, strict, or even too direct, it is but to motivate readers to awaken to their full potential as parents. I have applied the same technique of love and law to you as I have encouraged you to apply to your children.

It is also my happy experience that when parents are consistent and loving in their application of love and law, miracles happen throughout their parenting. Previously difficult, unruly, angry, and fearful children turn into happy and strong children! That is what makes me tick!

Parents who hated each other ended up forgiving each other, allowing peace and sometimes love to re-enter their hearts. That is my motivation and what brings me happiness.

I sincerely hope that I have been of service to you with this book. And remember: in all parenting (as in life itself), this will always be of use:

Know Your ABCs

- Avoid bad company
- Always be careful
- Always be cheerful
- Always be content

And for my Spiritual and/or Religious Readers:
Remember your ABCDEFG

Always Be Careful, Don't Ever Forget God!

# POINTS TO PONDER

*Make an action plan.*
*Write down what it is that appeals to*
*you from a chapter or from the book*
*as a whole. Make a note of what you*
*feel can help you in your parenting.*
*Make an action plan in which*
*you write down the steps that*
*you are going to take and how*
*to stick to them.*
*This has a tremendously positive impact.*
*First, because in doing so, this makes*
*you an active participant in what you*
*have read and learned, and second,*
*because the action plan will enable*
*you to develop your skills.*
*Evaluate by yourself and/or with your*
*partner what you have done with*
*the suggestions in each chapter.*
*Evaluate which changes you see*
*in yourself, each other, and*
*in your parenting.*
*And most of all, evaluate the*
*positive changes in your*
*children and enjoy them!*
*Be happy!*

For my free Parenting Tips, for the free eBook I co-author "Successful Living, Successful Relationships", and for a free download of my chapter in the book I co-authored with Brian Tracy join me at:

www.oopstheparentinghandbook.com

and visit me on Facebook at:

https://www.facebook.com/oopsparenting

# About the Author

Erik holds a degree in educational psychology from the University of Amsterdam.

Erik has won a Quilly Best Seller Award for the book he co-authored with Expert and Best Seller Author Brian Tracy.

Erik's successful career with many non-profit institutions in education, health care, and care for the mentally and physically impaired, culminated in an equally successful counselling practice for parenting.

He created the acclaimed Love and Law model of Parenting, cofounded the Learning with Heart and Soul Conferences, and represented The Netherlands in an EU international educational/parenting project from 2008 to 2010.

Erik travels extensively all over the world and considers the US and India his second homes.

Ten percent of his profits go to projects that offer direct help to the poorest of India with free health care, education, and clean water. He is also a supporter of Tibetan monks and nuns living in exile in India.

Join Erik at:
www.oopstheparentinghandbook.com

# Additional Reading

*Here are some of the works that have helped me to develop my views on parenting practices.*

Professor Joseph *Chilton Pearce: Evolution's End*

Woudstra, Verhulst, and de Witte: Kinder-en jeugdpsychiatrie

Dr Pal Dhall: Human Values Parenting

Sathya Sai Baba: *Educare: Human Values in Education*; Sathya Sai Speaks, volume 13

J. Krishnamurti: *The Future Is Now*

Professor J. Hawley: *Reawakening the Spirit in Work*

Webster-Stratton and Herbert: *Troubled Families*

E. Aron: *The Highly Sensitive Person*

Dr H.Q. Röling: *De tragedie van het geslachtsleven*

De Wit, Van der Veer, and Slot: *Psychologie van de Adolescentie*

Seifert and Hoffnung: *Child & Adolescent*

Dr S. Sandweiss: *With Love Man Is God*

Dr Frans Plooij: *Oei ik groei*

Drs. Erik R. Robertson: *Het Kan Anders*

*And many countless online documents and conferences regarding parenting and education*